D0527449

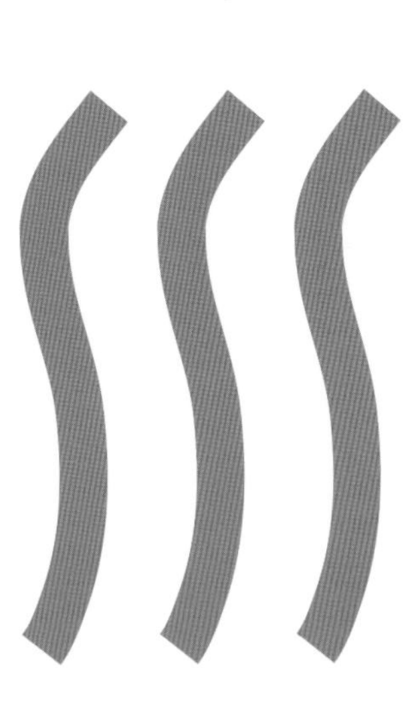

steam it

MURDOCH BOOKS

contents

what is steaming?

As the name suggests, steaming is a cooking method that uses moist heat or steam to cook food. The steam is created either by placing the food in a closed environment over boiling liquid so it cooks in the scalding vapour, or by enclosing the food in a parcel and letting it cook in its own juices. Either way, the end result is deliciously moist and tender. In addition, there are significant health benefits associated with steaming. The self-contained nature of the cooking method means that essential nutrients are more likely to be retained in the food compared with boiling, for example, where water-soluble vitamins and minerals can be leached away in the cooking liquid. There is also generally no need to add oil or fat to the food, which gives a lighter dish that is lower in fat and high on flavour.

steaming on the stovetop

By far the most popular way to steam is by putting the food in a steamer basket and steaming it over a saucepan or wok of boiling liquid. This method is both simple and effective, but there are a few things to bear in mind. Make sure the saucepan or wok is not filled with too much liquid as it can boil up into the steamer basket, spoiling the food and making a soggy mess. Aim to keep the pan one-third full. And make sure you use a steamer that fits well on the pan of liquid and has a tight-fitting lid to prevent steam escaping. If you are using a wok, check first that it balances well on the stovetop to avoid nasty spills — it may be worth investing in a wok stand to be on the safe side.

It is most common to sit the steamer over rapidly boiling water so that enough steam is generated to cook the food. However, some recipes steam over a more gentle heat; this is to prevent the food from toughening too quickly and results in a softer texture.

Steaming is quite a delicate way of cooking so, depending on what you're cooking, it can take up to one and a half times as long as simmering. It's worth checking the food and liquid levels regularly until you are more familiar with steaming. You will be rewarded with a dish that retains the inherent taste, shape and texture of the ingredients.

A word of warning too about the steam itself, which can cause serious scalding if caution is not used. Use the lid of the steamer as a shield, pointing away from you, when you are checking the food during steaming, and take care when removing the cooked food. Turn off the heat and use a tea towel (dish towel) or oven gloves to protect your hands.

steaming by absorption

This is a one-pot method of steaming on the stovetop. The correct amount of liquid is added to the food and left to simmer gently until all the liquid has been absorbed and the food is cooked. It's important to have a tight-fitting lid so that no steam can escape.

oven steaming

Oven-steaming is a very simple cooking method that results in fabulously tasty and tender food. Basically the food is wrapped and then steamed in its own juices in the oven. It can be wrapped in a variety of things — from foil and baking paper to banana leaves and even paperbark. Using leaves and bark not only gives a visual appeal to the dish, it also imparts a subtle flavour into the food. Of course, these wraps can be used when steaming on the stovetop as well.

Oven bags are a popular way of steaming in the oven. The added bonus with these is that you can put the meat, fish or chicken in the bag, throw in all the flavourings, close the bag, mix it all together and pop it in the oven. One-pot cooking without even using a pot!

For slow, gentle oven steaming, a water bath is often used, particularly for desserts. This method helps to protect the food from the heat. To create a water bath, all you need to do is put the cooking container (such as a cake tin, ramekin or mould) in a deep roasting tin and pour hot water into the tin to come halfway up the sides of the container. The food is then covered with foil to act as a lid which helps create steam.

types of steamers

Asian bamboo steamers are cheap and effective and look good enough to double as a serving plate. They come in a range of sizes, but make sure you choose one that fits snugly over the pan you will be cooking in (either a wok or large saucepan) without touching the water. The beauty of these steamers is that they are stackable with matching lids so you can cook various components of the meal at the same time.

Bamboo steamers need to be soaked in water for 15 minutes before being used for the first time. This will remove any excess odour that may taint the food during cooking. After use, wash them in hot soapy water and then leave to air-dry thoroughly before storing (especially when cooking strong-smelling food such as fish), otherwise they can become mildewed.

Metal steamers are made from aluminium or stainless steel and come in several sections: the bottom part for the cooking liquid; a separate compartment with holes that fits snugly over the top for the food; and a tight-fitting lid. Some brands have tiers, so several foods can be cooked at the same time. Although these steamers are more durable and easier to maintain, they are more expensive to buy and don't necessarily share the aesthetic appeal of the bamboo steamers.

Electric steamers are becoming more widely available. Usually made from a lightweight but durable plastic, they have a separate compartment for the water, and tiered baskets for the food. The advantage with this type of steamer is that you can fill the tiers with food, set the timer and leave it. The steamer will cook the food according to your instructions, then automatically switch off after the set cooking time.

Another idea is to use a heatproof dish instead of a steamer basket, which you rest on a round cake rack that will fit inside a wok or large saucepan (again, you must allow enough room underneath so the dish doesn't touch the water). Marinate the food for about 10 minutes (try ingredients such as soy sauce, lemon zest, ginger, garlic and sesame oil) then put the dish on the cake rack and cover. The steam dilutes the marinade flavours and forms a light sauce. To make sure the dish doesn't crack during steaming you may need to temper it. To do this, put a cake rack in a wok or saucepan and sit the dish on top. Add enough water to completely cover the dish, cover with a lid and bring the water to the boil. Boil for about 10 minutes, then remove from the heat and allow the water to cool to room temperature. You only need to do this once — the dish is now tempered for life.

hot tips for steaming

Regardless of whether you are using a metal or bamboo steamer, if you are cooking in stacks, make sure the most delicate or quickest-cooking ingredients are placed in the top rack, and the longer-cooking ingredients in the bottom rack where they will be closer to the heat and steam. If you are cooking large quantities of the same dish in stacks, swap them over halfway through cooking so the food cooks evenly. If you can't do this for some reason, make sure you give the top rack a longer cooking time.

To stop the food from sticking to the bottom of the steamer, either oil it or line it (lining it will also prevent the food from absorbing the bamboo smell). Baking paper makes an effective lining; it's usually worth pricking it with a skewer or the point of a sharp knife to allow the steam to come through into the steamer. Banana leaves are another option and are more visually appealing if you will be taking the steamer basket to the table.

Fill the wok or saucepan one-third full of boiling water, or pour in cold water and bring to the boil, then reduce the heat and keep it at a fast simmer. Don't overfill it, but it's just as important not to underfill it and allow the water to run dry. If more water is needed, especially with longer-cooking dishes, have some boiling water at hand so that you can replenish at any time without disturbing the cooking process.

For a subtle flavour boost, aromatic ingredients can be added to the steaming water. Take your pick from fresh herbs, spices, ginger, chopped root vegetables, lemon grass stems, thickly sliced onion, lemon or lime wedges, white wine — the list goes on. Whatever you choose, the natural flavours will mingle with the rising steam and complement the food in the steamer. And if you're seriously impressed with your creation, allow the liquid to cool, then put it in the refrigerator and use it for another meal.

Always try to arrange the food in the steamer in a single layer so that it cooks evenly — this is particularly important when cooking meat, chicken and seafood. If you are cooking in quantities too large to fit in a single layer, steam in batches rather than overcrowding the steamer. Another tip for even cooking is to cut the food into similar-sized pieces, remembering that larger pieces will take longer to cook.

Keep in mind that even when the steamer has been removed from the heat, the food will continue to cook. To avoid overcooked food, remove it from the steamer the minute it is ready or, if you are serving the food in the steamer, serve it straight away. As with any kind of cooking, leave meat and fish to rest off the heat for 5 minutes before serving — this helps retain moisture and will also make carving easier.

bamboo steamer

Bamboo steamers are inexpensive and come in a variety of sizes. You can use them for cooking a wide range of foods, and they also make attractive serving vessels.

metal steamer

Made from stainless steel or aluminium, these steamers are very durable and easy to maintain. Like bamboo steamers, they have multiple tiers and come in a range of sizes.

electric steamer

Electric steamers are becoming more popular, and this is largely due to the timer option. Food placed in the steamer ahead of time is cooked according to your specifications, then the steamer automatically switches off.

linings

Lining the steamer will prevent food sticking to the bottom. You can use baking paper (often pricked with holes to let the steam in) or banana leaves. These can also be used to wrap the food before steaming to keep it moist.

steaming techniques

Bamboo steamers should be **soaked** in water for 15 minutes before you use them for the **first time**.

To **prevent** food from sticking to the steamer, line the base with **baking paper** or banana leaves.

Fill the **wok** or saucepan one-third full of **water** and bring to the boil. If you put too much in, it will **boil up** and spoil the food.

It is important to arrange the food in a **single layer** so that it cooks evenly. Larger **quantities** can be cooked in batches.

starters

baby cos vietnamese chicken cups

makes 8

300 g (10 1/2 oz) skinless, boneless **chicken breast**
4 **spring onions (scallions)**, finely sliced
1 large handful **coriander (cilantro) leaves**
1 handful **mint**, torn
1 ripe but firm **mango**, flesh cut into thin strips
1 **Lebanese (short) cucumber**, seeded and cut into thin strips
2 tablespoons toasted **peanuts**
2 tablespoons **fried shallots** (see tip)
2 **baby cos (romaine) lettuces**, gently separated into 8 cups and rinsed

dressing

1 **garlic clove**, crushed
1 large **red chilli**, seeded and finely chopped
1 **lemon grass stem**, white part only, finely chopped
1 tablespoon grated fresh **ginger**
2 tablespoons **lime juice**
2 tablespoons **fish sauce**
2 teaspoons **caster (superfine) sugar**

Line the base of a steamer with baking paper and punch with holes. Place the chicken in the steamer in a single layer and cover securely with a lid. Sit the steamer over a wok or saucepan of boiling water and steam for 5–7 minutes, or until cooked when tested with a skewer. Remove the chicken and set aside on a plate to cool.

Meanwhile, put the spring onion, coriander, mint, mango, cucumber, peanuts and fried shallots in a large bowl. Shred the cooled chicken and add to the mixture.

To make the dressing, combine the garlic, chilli, lemon grass, ginger, lime juice, fish sauce, sugar and 1 tablespoon of water in a bowl and whisk until the sugar has dissolved. Pour the dressing over the chicken mixture and toss it through.

Spoon heaped tablespoons of the chicken mixture into the base of each lettuce cup and serve immediately.

tip **Fried shallots are available from Asian food shops or in the Asian section of larger supermarkets.**

pork balls wrapped in betel leaves

serves 6–8

375 g (13 oz) **minced (ground) pork**
1 heaped tablespoon **red curry paste**
1 **egg**, lightly beaten
2 **spring onions (scallions)**, finely chopped
1 **lemon grass stem**, white part only, finely chopped
2 **garlic cloves**, crushed
1 x 4 cm (1/2 x 1 1/2 inch) piece **ginger**, finely chopped
1 large **red chilli**, seeded and finely chopped
3 tablespoons chopped **coriander (cilantro) leaves**
85 g (3 oz/2/3 cup) finely sliced **green beans**
1 teaspoon **sesame oil**

dressing

2 tablespoons **sweet chilli sauce**
2 tablespoons **lime juice**
2 tablespoons **fish sauce**
1 tablespoon grated **palm sugar** or **soft brown sugar**

to serve

40 **betel leaves** (see tip)
3 tablespoons **fried shallots**
1 handful **coriander (cilantro) leaves**

Roll the mixture into walnut-sized balls, then **brush** each one lightly with sesame oil.

Arrange the **betel leaves** on each plate so your guests can make their own **wraps**.

Line the base of a large steamer with baking paper and punch with holes.

Put the pork, curry paste, egg, spring onion, lemon grass, garlic, ginger, chilli, coriander, beans and 1 teaspoon of salt in a large bowl and mix until well combined. Roll the mixture into walnut-sized balls then brush each ball lightly with sesame oil (alternatively, put a few drops of oil on your hands and roll them — replenish the oil every 3–4 balls). Place the balls in the prepared steamer and cover with a lid. Sit the steamer over a wok or saucepan of boiling water and steam for 10 minutes, or until cooked. Transfer to a serving bowl.

Meanwhile, to make the dressing, put the sweet chilli sauce, lime juice, fish sauce and sugar in a bowl and stir until well combined and the sugar has dissolved.

Put a stack of betel leaves on each serving plate so that your guests can make their own wraps. Place a pork ball on the matte side of the leaf, top with some fried shallots and coriander leaves and drizzle with the dressing. Delicious served with an ice-cold beer.

tip **Betel leaves, also known as wild betel leaves or cha plu, are tender, bright green leaves with a delicate but distinctive flavour. They are sold in bunches at speciality fruit and vegetable shops and Asian shops. If you can't find them, use witlof (chicory/Belgian endive) leaves.**

basil and leek ravioli

serves 4

25 g (1 oz) **butter**
1 **leek**, white part only, cut lengthways and finely sliced
200 g (7 oz) **ricotta cheese**
25 g (1 oz/1/4 cup) grated **parmesan cheese**
1 handful **basil**, torn
3 tablespoons **pine nuts**, toasted
24 **round gow gee dumpling wrappers**

tomato salsa

2 vine-ripened **tomatoes**
boiling **water**
1 small handful **basil**, torn
2 tablespoons **garlic-infused olive oil** (see tip)

Line the base of two steamers with baking paper and punch with holes. Melt the butter in a large frying pan over medium–low heat and cook the leek for 10 minutes, or until softened but not coloured. Remove the leek from the pan and allow to cool in a bowl. Combine the ricotta, parmesan, basil and pine nuts in a large bowl and season with salt and ground pepper. Add the cooled leeks and toss to combine.

Lay 12 gow gee wrappers out on a clean surface. Place a heaped tablespoon of the mixture in the middle of each wrapper, leaving a 2 cm (3/4 inch) border. Brush the border with water and place a second wrapper on top. Press down securely around the edges to prevent any filling spilling out.

Arrange the ravioli in a single layer in the steamers. Brush generously with water on both sides then cover with a lid. Sit the steamers over a saucepan or wok of boiling water and steam for 15 minutes, brushing once with water halfway through cooking.

To make the salsa, score a cross in the base of the tomatoes. Put in a heatproof bowl and cover with boiling water. Leave for 30 seconds, then transfer to cold water and peel away the skin from the cross. Cut the tomatoes in half, scoop out the seeds, then finely chop the flesh. Toss together the tomato, basil and oil. Arrange three ravioli on each serving plate and spoon on some of the salsa.

tip **Garlic-infused olive oil is available at delicatessens and gourmet food stores. If you can't find it, warm some olive oil with a couple of sliced garlic cloves, then leave to cool and strain.**

pork buns

makes 12

dough

2 tablespoons **sugar**

1 1/2 teaspoons **dried yeast**

310 g (11 oz/2 1/2 cups) **plain (all-purpose) flour**

1 tablespoon **vegetable oil**

1/2 teaspoon **sesame oil**

1 1/2 teaspoons **baking powder**

1 teaspoon **vegetable oil**

250 g (9 oz) **Chinese barbecued pork**, finely chopped

2 tablespoons **oyster sauce**

2 teaspoons **sugar**

2 teaspoons **Chinese rice wine**

1 teaspoon **sesame oil**

1 teaspoon **soy sauce**

To make the dough, pour 250 ml (9 fl oz/1 cup) of warm water into a small bowl and add the sugar. Stir for a few seconds to dissolve the sugar then add the yeast. Cover the bowl and leave for 10 minutes.

Sift the flour into a bowl and make a well in the centre. Pour the yeast mixture and vegetable oil into the well. Quickly stir the ingredients together and turn the mixture out onto a lightly floured surface. Knead for 8 minutes, or until smooth and elastic. Brush a large bowl with the sesame oil and put the dough in the bowl, turning it around in the bowl to coat it all with the oil. Cover the bowl and set aside to rise for at least 3 hours.

Lift the dough onto a lightly floured work surface. Punch the dough down and flatten into a large round. Sprinkle the baking powder in the centre of the circle, bringing the edges up towards the centre. Firmly press the edges together, then knead the dough for a further 5 minutes. Divide the dough into 12 equal portions and roll into balls. Cover with a damp cloth to prevent them from drying out.

To make the filling, heat a wok over high heat, add the oil and swirl to coat. Add the pork and cook for 30 seconds, stirring constantly. Add the oyster sauce, sugar, rice wine, sesame oil and soy sauce and stir-fry for 1–2 minutes. Transfer the mixture to a bowl to cool.

Take each ball of dough and press it onto a lightly floured surface to form a circle 12 cm (4 1/2 inches) in diameter. Place a heaped tablespoon of the filling in the centre of each dough circle, then bring the edges up to the centre. Press the edges firmly together. Sit each bun on a 5 cm (2 inch) square piece of baking paper.

Place six pork buns on each layer of a double steamer and cover with a lid. Sit the steamer over a wok or saucepan of boiling water and steam for 15 minutes. Serve warm.

Pour the **yeast** mixture and vegetable oil into the **sifted flour** and quickly stir together.

Put a heaped teaspoon of **filling** in the centre of each dough circle, then bring the edges up to the centre.

mini zucchini, baby spinach and goat's cheese frittatas

makes 6

5 large **eggs**

170 ml ($5\frac{1}{2}$ fl oz/$\frac{2}{3}$ cup) **cream (whipping)**

$\frac{1}{2}$ teaspoon freshly grated **nutmeg**

1 tablespoon **olive oil**

2 **spring onions (scallions)**, finely chopped

150 g ($5\frac{1}{2}$ oz/3 cups) **baby English spinach**

3 tablespoons chopped **flat-leaf (Italian) parsley**

3 small **zucchini (courgettes)**, halved lengthways and finely sliced

100 g ($3\frac{1}{2}$ oz) soft **goat's cheese**, crumbled

2 tablespoons **flat-leaf (Italian) parsley**, extra

2 tablespoons shaved **parmesan cheese**

Preheat the oven to 180°C (350°F/Gas 4). Lightly grease a 6-hole giant muffin tin and line the bases with baking paper.

Beat the eggs, cream, nutmeg and salt and pepper in a large bowl, then set aside. Heat the olive oil in a large frying pan over medium heat and cook the spring onion for 3 minutes, or until soft and translucent. Increase the heat to high, add the baby spinach and parsley and allow to wilt. Remove from the heat and leave to cool for 5 minutes.

When cool, add the onion and spinach to the egg mixture, then stir in the zucchini. Pour the mixture into the muffin holes, then dollop the goat's cheese into each one so the cheese is more or less submerged in the filling. Place the tray in a large, deep baking tin and pour in enough hot water to come halfway up the side of the muffin tin. Cover the baking tin with a large sheet of foil and steam in the oven for 40 minutes, or until set.

Allow the frittatas to cool in the tin for 5 minutes, then carefully remove them with a small spatula, or invert onto a clean board. Place the frittatas on serving plates then arrange some parsley leaves and parmesan shavings on top.

rice noodle rolls filled with prawns

serves 4

sauce

140 g (5 oz/1/2 cup) **sesame paste** (see tip)

4 tablespoons **light soy sauce**

3 tablespoons **lime juice**

3 tablespoons grated **palm sugar** or **soft brown sugar**

1 tablespoon **sesame oil**

2 tablespoons **peanut oil**

1 teaspoon **sesame oil**

4 **garlic cloves**, finely chopped

5 **spring onions (scallions)**, finely sliced

150 g (5 1/2 oz/1 large bunch) **garlic chives**, cut into 2 cm (3/4 inch) lengths

165 g (5 3/4 oz/1 cup) **water chestnuts**, finely sliced

3 tablespoons **sesame seeds**, lightly toasted

500 g (1 lb 2 oz) fresh **rice sheet noodles**

800 g (1 lb 12 oz) small **raw prawns (shrimp)**, peeled and deveined

50 g (1 3/4 oz/1/3 cup) **unsalted peanuts**, crushed

Add the spring onion and garlic chives and cook until **softened**.

Place four **prawns** on top of the chive mixture and roll up the **noodle sheet** tightly.

To make the sauce, combine the sesame paste, soy sauce, lime juice, palm sugar and sesame oil in a bowl and stir until the sugar has dissolved and the sauce is smooth. Add a tablespoon of water if it appears to be a little too thick.

Heat the peanut oil and sesame oil in a frying pan, add the garlic and cook for 1 minute. Add the spring onion and garlic chives and cook for about 2 minutes, or until softened. Add the water chestnuts and sesame seeds. Remove from the heat and allow to cool.

Unroll the noodle sheets and cut into eight 15 x 17 cm (6 x 6 1/2 inch) pieces. Put 1 tablespoon of the chive mixture along one long end. Place four prawns, curled up, side by side, on top of the chive mixture and roll up the noodle sheet tightly, then sit it on a plate that will fit inside a steamer. Repeat with the remaining rolls and filling ingredients. Lay the rolls side by side in two layers, with a layer of baking paper in between the rolls to stop them sticking together.

Place the plate in a steamer and cover with a lid. Sit the steamer over a wok or saucepan of simmering water and steam for 10 minutes, or until the prawns turn opaque and are cooked.

Carefully lift the plate out of the steamer with a tea towel (dish towel) and drizzle some of the sauce over the top, and around the rolls, then sprinkle with the crushed peanuts. Serve extra sauce on the side.

tip **Sesame paste is a thick, brown paste made from sesame seeds, and should not be confused with the Middle Eastern paste, tahini. It is available from Asian food stores. Smooth peanut butter can be substituted but this will alter the flavour of the finished dish.**

prawn banana leaf cups

makes 8

16 x 10 cm (4 inch) circles of **banana leaf**

300 g (10 1/2 oz) **raw prawns (shrimp)**, peeled and deveined

1 small **red chilli**, seeded

2 teaspoons **Thai red curry paste**

3 cm (1 1/4 inch) piece of **lemon grass**, white part only, roughly chopped

1 large **egg**

3 tablespoons **coconut cream**

1 tablespoon **fish sauce**

1/4 teaspoon **sugar**

2 tablespoons **unsalted peanuts**

Place two banana leaf circles together to make a double layer. Make four small tucks around the circle, stapling them to secure as you go, to create a banana leaf 'cup'. Repeat to make eight cups in all. Alternatively you can use eight 100 ml (3 1/2 fl oz) ramekins and cut out eight 7 cm (2 3/4 inch) rounds of baking paper.

Tip the prawns into a food processor with the chilli, curry paste, lemon grass, egg, coconut cream, fish sauce, sugar and half the peanuts. Blend to a rough paste.

Evenly divide the mixture among the cups or ramekins, then place a round of baking paper on top of each one. Arrange in a single layer in a steamer (you may need to do this in batches) and cover with a lid. Sit the steamer over a wok or saucepan of simmering water and steam for 10–12 minutes, or until the mixture has risen and feels firm to the touch. Remove the baking paper.

Meanwhile, lightly toast the remaining peanuts. Cool a little, then roughly chop. Scatter over the prawn cups and serve.

thai fish cakes

makes 24

chilli lime dipping sauce

1 small **red chilli**, seeded and finely chopped

1 teaspoon **caster (superfine) sugar**

1 1/2 tablespoons **rice vinegar**

1 1/2 tablespoons **lime juice**

2 tablespoons **fish sauce**

1/4 small **carrot**, finely chopped

1/4 small **Lebanese (short) cucumber**, seeded and finely chopped

600 g (1 lb 5 oz) skinless **firm white fish fillets** (such as ling, bream or redfish)

2 tablespoons **Thai red curry paste**

2 tablespoons **fish sauce**

3 teaspoons **lime juice**

1 **egg**, lightly beaten

2 tablespoons finely chopped **coriander (cilantro) leaves and roots**

4 **makrut (kaffir lime) leaves**, finely chopped

150 g (5 1/2 oz) **snake (yard-long) beans**, finely chopped

24 **mint leaves**

To make the dipping sauce, combine all the ingredients and 3 tablespoons of water in a bowl and stir until the sugar has dissolved and the ingredients are well combined.

Put the fish, curry paste, fish sauce and lime juice in a food processor and blend until a smooth, sticky paste is formed. Transfer to a large non-metallic bowl and add the egg, coriander, lime leaves, snake beans and 1/2 teaspoon of salt. Using your hands, mix until the ingredients are well combined.

Line a large steamer with baking paper and punch with holes. Shape tablespoons of the fish mixture into 24 small balls, then flatten gently with the palm of your hand to form patties. Arrange the patties in the steamer, making sure they don't touch each other (use a second steamer if necessary). Put a mint leaf on top of each patty and cover the steamer with a lid. Sit the steamer over a wok or saucepan of simmering water and steam for 10–12 minutes, or until cooked through. Remove from the heat and serve immediately with the chilli lime dipping sauce.

Combine the **dipping** sauce ingredients and stir until the sugar has **dissolved**.

Shape the mixture into balls, then **flatten** gently to form patties.

black figs with goat's cheese wrapped in prosciutto

serves 4

8 large **black figs**

80 g (2 3/4 oz) soft **goat's cheese**

8 thin slices of **prosciutto**

2 tablespoons **lemon oil** (see tip)

2 tablespoon chopped **pistachio nuts**

Line a steamer with baking paper and punch with holes. Cut the figs into quarters almost to the base so that they still keep together, then carefully stuff small chunks of goat's cheese into each fig.

Place the stuffed figs in the prepared steamer and cover with a lid. Sit the steamer over a saucepan or wok of boiling water and steam for 5–8 minutes, or until the figs are tender and the cheese is warm, but still holds its shape.

Carefully wrap a slice of prosciutto around each fig, then season well with freshly ground black pepper and drizzle with the lemon oil. Sprinkle the pistachios over the top before serving.

tip **Lemon oil is available from good delicatessens and gourmet food stores. If you can't find it, use extra virgin olive oil flavoured with the grated zest of a lemon.**

vine leaves stuffed with spinach and pistachios

makes 30

4 tablespoons **extra virgin olive oil**
330 g ($11\frac{1}{2}$ oz) **English spinach**, leaves removed and finely chopped
8 **bulb spring onions (scallions)**, finely chopped (include the green parts)
2 **garlic cloves**, crushed
220 g ($7\frac{3}{4}$ oz/1 cup) **risotto rice** (such as arborio)
1 teaspoon **ground cumin**
2 tablespoons chopped **flat-leaf (Italian) parsley**
2 tablespoons chopped **mint**
40 g ($1\frac{1}{2}$ oz/$\frac{1}{3}$ cup) **sultanas (golden raisins)**
50 g ($1\frac{3}{4}$ oz/$\frac{1}{3}$ cup) **pistachio nuts**, roughly chopped
juice of 1 **lemon**
670 ml (23 fl oz/$2\frac{2}{3}$ cups) boiling **water**
30 **preserved vine leaves**, rinsed well and drained
lemon wedges, to serve
ready-made **tzatziki**, to serve

Line a 28 cm ($11\frac{1}{4}$ inch) spring-form cake tin with baking paper. Heat 1 tablespoon of the oil in a large frying pan over medium–high heat. Add the spinach and sauté for 3 minutes, or until wilted. Remove from the pan and set aside in a bowl to cool.

Heat 2 tablespoons of oil in the same frying pan over medium heat and cook the spring onion until soft but not coloured. Add the garlic, cook for 1 minute then add the rice, cumin, parsley, mint, sultanas, pistachios, lemon juice and 500 ml (17 fl oz/ 2 cups) of boiling water. Remove any excess water from the spinach and add to the pan, season well, then cover and simmer for 10 minutes. The rice should be half cooked and have soaked up all the liquid.

Place each vine leaf, shiny side down, on a board and add 2 heaped teaspoons of the filling. Roll up, turning in the sides to make neat, well-sealed parcels. Arrange the parcels, join side down, in a single layer in the tin. Pour the remaining boiling water and oil over the parcels, then put a plate on top to stop the parcels unravelling. Put the cake tin in a 30 cm (12 inch) steamer and cover with a lid. Sit the steamer over a saucepan or wok of boiling water and steam for 45 minutes, or until the rice is tender and has absorbed most of the liquid. Add more boiling water to the pan as needed. Serve the parcels at room temperature with lemon wedges and tzatziki.

tuna and cannellini bean pâté with garlic crostini

serves 4–6

150 g (5 1/2 oz/3/4 cup) **cannellini beans**, soaked in water overnight, drained
1 **bay leaf**
2 x 150 g (5 1/2 oz) **tuna steaks**
150 ml (5 fl oz) **garlic-infused olive oil**, plus extra, to serve
1/2 small **red onion**, finely chopped
3 tablespoons finely chopped **flat-leaf (Italian) parsley**
1 tablespoon chopped **thyme**
2 teaspoons **lemon zest**
2 tablespoons **lemon juice**
sea salt, to taste

garlic crostini

1 loaf **pide (Turkish/flat bread)**
3 tablespoons **garlic-infused olive oil**

Put the cannellini beans, bay leaf and 625 ml (21 1/2 fl oz/2 1/2 cups) of water in a saucepan over high heat and bring to the boil. Reduce the heat and simmer, covered, for 1 hour, or until the beans are tender but not falling apart. Drain the beans into a colander and rinse with cold water. Discard the bay leaf.

Meanwhile, put the tuna steaks on a plate and place in a 30 cm (12 inch) steamer. Cover with a lid and sit the steamer over a saucepan or wok of boiling water. Steam for 4–5 minutes, or until the tuna is almost cooked but is still pink in the centre. Remove the tuna from the steamer and drizzle with 3 tablespoons of garlic-infused olive oil. Cool to room temperature, then flake the flesh with a fork.

Put the onion, parsley, thyme, lemon zest, lemon juice, sea salt and freshly ground black pepper in a large bowl and add the cannellini beans. With the back of a fork gently crush the beans, then add the tuna and remaining oil and toss gently to combine. Spoon the pâté into small bowls, garnish with ground black pepper and drizzle with a little extra garlic oil.

Preheat the oven to 160°C (315°F/Gas 2–3) and line two baking trays with baking paper. Cut the bread into 1 cm (1/2 inch) thick slices. Lightly brush each side of the bread with the garlic oil, then arrange on the baking trays. Bake for 15 minutes, or until lightly golden brown, then turn over and bake for a further 15 minutes. Allow the crostini to cool, then serve with the pâté.

california rolls

makes 30

500 g (1 lb 2 oz/2 1/2 cups) **short-grain white rice**

3 tablespoons **rice vinegar**

1 tablespoon **caster (superfine) sugar**

5 sheets of **nori**

1 **Lebanese (short) cucumber**, cut lengthways into long batons

1 **avocado**, finely sliced

1 tablespoon **black sesame seeds**, toasted

30 g (1 oz) **pickled ginger slices**

125 g (4 1/2 oz/1/2 cup) **mayonnaise**

3 teaspoons **wasabi paste**

2 teaspoons **soy sauce**

Wash the rice, then **cook** over low heat until **tunnels** form.

Using a **bamboo mat**, continue rolling the nori tightly to join the edge.

Wash the rice under cold running water, tossing, until the water runs clear. Put the rice and 750 ml (26 fl oz/3 cups) of water in a saucepan. Bring to the boil over low heat and cook for 5 minutes, or until tunnels form in the rice. Remove from the heat, cover and leave for 15 minutes.

Put the vinegar, sugar and 1 teaspoon of salt in a small saucepan and stir over low heat until the sugar and salt have dissolved.

Transfer the rice to a non-metallic bowl and use a wooden spoon to separate the grains. Make a slight well in the centre, slowly stir in the vinegar dressing, then leave to cool a little.

Lay a nori sheet, shiny side down, on a bamboo mat or flat surface and spread out one-fifth of the rice, leaving a narrow border at one end. Arrange one-fifth of the cucumber, avocado, sesame seeds and ginger lengthways over the rice, keeping away from the border. Spread with some of the combined mayonnaise, wasabi and soy sauce and roll to cover the filling. Continue rolling tightly to join the edge, then hold it in place for a few seconds. Trim the ends and cut into slices. Repeat with the remaining nori sheets and filling and serve with the remaining wasabi mayonnaise.

mussels in chunky tomato sauce

serves 6

1.5 kg (3 lb 5 oz) **black mussels**

1 tablespoon **olive oil**

1 large **onion**, diced

4 **garlic cloves**, finely chopped

800 g (1 lb 12 oz) tinned **chopped tomatoes**

3 tablespoons **tomato paste (concentrated purée)**

30 g (1 oz/1/4 cup) pitted **black olives**

1 tablespoon **capers**, rinsed and squeezed dry

125 ml (4 fl oz/1/2 cup) **fish stock**

3 tablespoons chopped **flat-leaf (Italian) parsley**

Scrub the mussels with a stiff brush and pull out the hairy beards. Discard any damaged mussels, or any that don't close when tapped on the bench.

In a large saucepan, heat the olive oil and cook the onion and garlic over medium heat for 1–2 minutes, or until softened. Add the tomato, tomato paste, olives, capers and fish stock. Bring to the boil, then reduce the heat and simmer, stirring occasionally, for 20 minutes, or until the sauce is thick.

Stir in the mussels and cover the saucepan. Shake or toss the mussels occasionally and cook for 4–5 minutes, or until the mussels begin to open. Remove the pan from the heat and discard any mussels that haven't opened in the cooking time. Add the parsley, toss gently and serve.

sweet potato and red lentil dip

serves 6–8

250 g (9 oz) **orange sweet potato**, roughly chopped

1 tablespoon **olive oil**

1 small **red onion**, finely chopped

1 **garlic clove**, crushed

1 teaspoon grated fresh **ginger**

1 tablespoon **Thai red curry paste**

200 g (7 oz) tinned **diced tomatoes**

125 g (4 1/2 oz/1/2 cup) **whole red lentils**, rinsed (see tip)

375 ml (13 fl oz/1 1/2 cups) **chicken stock**

Put the sweet potato in a steamer and cover with a lid. Sit the steamer over a wok or saucepan of boiling water and steam for 15 minutes, or until tender. Transfer to a bowl, cool and mash roughly with a fork.

Heat the oil in a saucepan over medium heat and cook the onion for 2 minutes, or until softened. Add the garlic, ginger and curry paste and stir for 30 seconds.

Add the tomatoes, lentils and stock to the pan. Bring to the boil, then reduce the heat to low, cover and simmer, stirring often, for 30 minutes, or until the mixture thickens and the lentils have softened but are still intact. Spoon the mixture into a bowl, refrigerate until cold, then carefully stir into the mashed sweet potato with a fork. Season to taste with salt and freshly ground black pepper. Serve with pitta bread wedges, savoury crackers or crusty bread for dipping.

tip **If you are using split red lentils for this recipe, reduce the cooking time to 10–15 minutes and don't cover with a lid.**

sugar cane prawns

makes 10

500 g (1 lb 2 oz) **raw prawns (shrimp)**, peeled, deveined and roughly chopped
2 tablespoons chopped **coriander (cilantro) leaves**
2 tablespoons chopped **mint**
1 **lemon grass stem**, white part only, finely chopped
1 small **red chilli**, seeded and finely chopped
1 **garlic clove**, crushed
1 1/2 tablespoons **fish sauce**
2 teaspoons **lime juice**
1/2 teaspoon **sugar**
10 pieces of **sugar cane**, about 10 cm (4 inches) long and 5 mm (1/4 inch) wide (see tip)
lime wedges, to serve

Put the prawns, coriander, mint, lemon grass, chilli, garlic, fish sauce, lime juice, sugar and 1/4 teaspoon of salt in a food processor and blend until smooth.

With wet hands, roll 2 tablespoons of the mixture into a ball, then mould around the middle of a sugar cane skewer, pressing firmly to secure onto the skewer. Repeat with the remaining mixture and sugar cane, then refrigerate for 15 minutes.

Line a steamer with baking paper and punch with holes. Arrange the skewers on top in a single layer and cover with a lid. Sit the steamer over a wok or saucepan of boiling water and steam for 7–8 minutes, or until cooked through.

Serve the skewers with lime wedges or with a quick dipping sauce made up of sweet chilli sauce mixed with a little fish sauce.

tip **If you can't find fresh sugar cane, the tinned version is fine. Look for it in Asian food stores.**

mushroom and water chestnut steamed buns

makes 24

dough

600 g (1 lb 5 oz/4 3/4 cups) **plain (all-purpose) flour**

2 tablespoons **baking powder**

2 tablespoons **caster (superfine) sugar**

3 tablespoons **peanut oil**

2 tablespoons **oil**

2 **garlic cloves**, finely chopped

1 teaspoon finely grated fresh **ginger**

1 small **red chilli**, seeded and finely sliced

8 **Swiss brown mushrooms**, finely chopped

8 **shiitake mushrooms**, finely chopped

225 g (8 oz) tin **water chestnuts**, drained and finely chopped

2 tablespoons **oyster sauce**

1 tablespoon **soy sauce**

1 teaspoon **cornflour (cornstarch)** mixed with 1 tablespoon **water**

2 **spring onions (scallions)**, chopped

1 tablespoon chopped **coriander (cilantro) leaves**

To make the dough, sift the flour, baking powder, sugar and 1 teaspoon of salt into a bowl. Gradually stir in the oil and 375 ml (13 fl oz/1 1/2 cups) of water and mix to a soft dough. Turn the dough out onto a floured board and knead for 5 minutes, or until the dough is smooth and elastic. Cover and let the dough rest at room temperature for 1 hour.

Meanwhile, heat the oil in a frying pan over medium heat, add the garlic, ginger and chilli and cook for 1 minute, or until softened. Stir in all the mushrooms and cook for a further 5 minutes, or until the mushrooms are tender. Add the water chestnuts, oyster sauce, soy sauce and combined cornflour and water and simmer, stirring, for about 1 minute, or until the mixture has thickened slightly. Remove from the heat and stir in the spring onion and coriander. Set aside to cool.

Divide the dough into 24 pieces. Shape each piece into a 6 cm (2 1/2 inch) flat round. Put 1 teaspoon of mushroom mixture in the centre of each and gather the edges together, pinching to enclose the filling.

Line a steamer with baking paper and punch with holes. Place the buns on top, 2 cm (3/4 inch) apart, and cover with a lid (you may need to do this in batches). Sit the steamer over a wok or saucepan of boiling water and steam for about 15–20 minutes, or until the buns are firm. Serve immediately.

Add the **mushrooms** to the garlic mixture and **cook** until tender.

Gather the dough edges together and **pinch** to enclose the filling.

chicken and rocket sausages with warm tomato sauce

makes 10

500 g (1 lb 2 oz) **minced (ground) chicken**
2 **spring onions (scallions)**, finely sliced
2 **garlic cloves**, finely chopped
50 g (1 3/4 oz/1/2 cup) shredded **parmesan cheese**
40 g (1 1/2 oz/1/2 cup) **fresh breadcrumbs**
40 g (1 1/2 oz/1 cup) shredded **baby rocket (arugula)**
1 **egg**, lightly beaten
2 tablespoons **olive oil**
1 **small onion**, finely chopped
3 **garlic cloves**, extra, finely chopped
400 g (14 oz) tin **chopped tomatoes**
2 teaspoons **sugar**
1 small handful **basil**, roughly chopped
5 slices of **prosciutto**, halved

Put the chicken, spring onion, garlic, cheese, breadcrumbs, rocket and egg in a bowl and mix well to combine. With wet hands form 2 heaped tablespoons of the mixture into a sausage shape. Lay on a tray and repeat with the remaining mixture to make 10 sausages. Cover and refrigerate for 1 hour.

Meanwhile, heat the oil in a saucepan over low heat and cook the onion and extra garlic for 5 minutes, or until softened. Add the tomatoes, sugar, half the basil and 125 ml (4 fl oz/1/2 cup) of water and season with salt and freshly ground black pepper. Bring to the boil, then reduce the heat and simmer for 15 minutes, or until the sauce has reduced and thickened slightly.

Line a steamer with baking paper and punch with holes. Arrange the sausages in a single layer on top and cover with a lid. Sit the steamer over a saucepan or wok of boiling water and steam for 15–20 minutes, or until the sausages are firm and cooked through. Remove the sausages and set aside to cool slightly.

Wrap a slice of prosciutto around each sausage, then place under a hot grill (broiler) for 3 minutes each side, or until slightly crisp. Serve with the warm tomato sauce and sprinkle the remaining basil over the top.

prawn nori rolls

makes 25 rolls

500 g (1 lb 2 oz) **raw prawns (shrimp)**, peeled and deveined

1 1/2 tablespoons **fish sauce**

1 tablespoon **sake**

2 tablespoons chopped **coriander (cilantro) leaves**

1 large **makrut (kaffir lime) leaf**, finely shredded

1 tablespoon **lime juice**

2 teaspoons **sweet chilli sauce**

1 **egg white**, lightly beaten

5 sheets of **nori**

dipping sauce

3 tablespoons **sake**

3 tablespoons **light soy sauce**

1 tablespoon **mirin**

1 tablespoon **lime juice**

Spread the **prawn** mixture over each sheet of nori and **roll up** tightly.

Arrange the nori rolls in a **single layer** in a steamer lined with baking **paper**.

Put the prawns, fish sauce, sake, coriander, lime leaf, lime juice and sweet chilli sauce in a food processor and blend until smooth. Add the egg white and pulse for a few seconds to just combine.

Lay the nori sheets on a flat surface, shiny side down, and spread some prawn mixture over each sheet, leaving a 2 cm (3/4 inch) border at one end. Roll up tightly, cover and refrigerate for 1 hour to firm. Using a sharp knife, trim the ends and cut into 2 cm (3/4 inch) lengths.

Line a steamer with baking paper and punch with holes. Arrange the rolls in the steamer in a single layer and cover with a lid. Sit the steamer over a wok or saucepan of boiling water and steam for 5 minutes, or until cooked.

To make the dipping sauce, mix together all the ingredients in a small bowl. Serve with the nori rolls.

eggplant and garlic dip

serves 6

1 large **eggplant (aubergine)**

2 tablespoons **olive oil**

2 tablespoons **lemon juice**

2 **garlic cloves**, finely chopped

2 tablespoons chopped **parsley**

1/4 teaspoon **ground cumin**

Line a steamer with baking paper and punch with holes. Lay the whole eggplant on top and cover with a lid. Sit the steamer over a saucepan or wok of boiling water and steam for 30–40 minutes, or until the eggplant is very soft. Check the water levels as you go, and replenish as needed. Remove the eggplant from the steamer and cool completely.

Combine the oil, lemon juice, garlic, parsley and cumin in a bowl. Halve the eggplant, scoop out the flesh and roughly chop it into the oil mixture, mashing lightly with a fork. Season well with salt and freshly ground black pepper.

Store in an airtight container and refrigerate until ready to serve. If you can, make this dip the day before to give the flavours time to develop fully. Serve with crackers or torn pieces of wood-fired bread.

pea and artichoke slice

serves 10 as a starter or 6 as a main

2 tablespoons **olive oil**

4 **garlic cloves**, chopped

3 **boiling potatoes**, diced

310 g (11 oz/2 cups) **frozen peas**

4 tablespoons **crème fraîche** or **sour cream**

3 **spring onions (scallions)**, roughly chopped

4 tablespoons roughly chopped **mint**

2 **eggs**, separated

800 g (1 lb 12 oz) tinned **artichokes**, drained (see tip)

1 tablespoon **lemon juice**

1 1/2 tablespoons **pine nuts**, toasted

25 g (1 oz/1/4 cup) grated **parmesan cheese**

baby salad leaves, to serve

1 tablespoon **extra virgin olive oil**

1 teaspoon **sherry vinegar**

Lightly grease a 20 x 7 x 10 cm (8 x 2 3/4 x 4 inch) loaf (bar) tin and line with baking paper. Line a steamer with baking paper and punch with holes.

Heat 1 tablespoon of olive oil in a small saucepan over medium heat and sauté the garlic for 2–3 minutes, or until fragrant. Remove from the heat. Put the potatoes and peas in the steamer and cover with a lid. Sit the steamer over a saucepan or wok of simmering water and steam for 10 minutes, or until the potato is cooked. Place in a food processor with the crème fraîche, spring onion, mint and half the garlic and process until smooth. Season well. Add the egg yolks and combine. Transfer to a large bowl.

In a clean separate bowl, beat the egg whites with electric beaters until firm peaks form, then gently fold into the pea mixture with a metal spoon. Spoon into the prepared tin and smooth the top.

Cover the loaf tin with foil, place in a large steamer and cover with a lid. Sit the steamer over a saucepan or wok of boiling water and steam for 30 minutes.

Put the artichokes, lemon juice, pine nuts, cheese and the remaining garlic in a food processor and blend until the mixture is smooth but textured. Season well.

Allow the potato and pea terrine to cool until warm or room temperature, then spread with the artichoke mixture. Gently lift from the tin using baking paper and cut into slices. Arrange one slice on each plate with a handful of salad leaves. Combine the olive oil and vinegar with salt and pepper in a small jar and drizzle around the plate.

tip **If you would rather use fresh artichokes you will need about 5 or 6 of them. Place them in a steamer, cover and steam over simmering water for 40–50 minutes, or until the outer leaves come off easily. When cool, remove the leaves and remove the choke.**

Using a metal spoon, **gently fold** the beaten egg white into the pea mixture.

Spread the **artichoke** mixture over the cooled **terrine** and smooth the surface.

chicken and pistachio dumplings

makes 20

300 g (10 1/2 oz) **minced (ground) chicken**
80 g (2 3/4 oz/1/2 cup) **unsalted pistachio nuts**, finely chopped
1 **garlic clove**, crushed
2 tablespoons chopped **mint**
1 tablespoon grated **lemon zest**
1/2 teaspoon **ground allspice**
1/4 teaspoon **ground cinnamon**
1/4 teaspoon **Tabasco sauce**
20 **round gow gee dumpling wrappers**

sauce
1 tablespoon **olive oil**
1 small **onion**, finely chopped
1 **red chilli**, seeded and finely chopped
2 **garlic cloves**, crushed
3 tablespoons **dry white wine**
400 g (14 oz) tin **chopped tomatoes**
1 **cinnamon stick**
1/2 teaspoon **Tabasco sauce** (optional)

Combine the chicken, pistachios, garlic, mint, lemon zest, allspice, cinnamon, Tabasco, 1/4 teaspoon of ground black pepper and some salt in a bowl. Spoon the mixture in the centre of the gow gee wrappers and bring the edges up around the filling, pleating as you go to encase the filling (leave the top open).

Line a steamer with baking paper and punch with holes. Place the dumplings in a single layer on top and cover with a lid. Sit the steamer over a wok or saucepan of boiling water and steam for 15 minutes, or until cooked. If the dumplings start to dry out during cooking, brush generously with water.

To make the sauce, heat the oil in a small saucepan over medium heat. Add the onion, chilli and garlic and cook, stirring, for 5 minutes, or until the onion has softened. Add the wine, tomatoes, cinnamon and Tabasco if using, bring to the boil, then reduce the heat and simmer, stirring occasionally, for about 15 minutes. Remove the cinnamon stick and transfer the sauce to a food processor. Blend until smooth, then season well.

To serve, spoon the sauce onto serving plates and place the dumplings on top, or arrange the dumplings on a platter and use the sauce for dipping.

asian oysters

serves 4

12 **oysters**, on the shell

2 **garlic cloves**, finely chopped

2 x 2 cm (3/4 x 3/4 inch) piece **ginger**, cut into julienne strips

2 **spring onions (scallions)**, finely sliced on the diagonal

3 tablespoons **Japanese soy sauce**

3 tablespoons **peanut oil**

coriander (cilantro) leaves, to garnish

Line a large steamer with baking paper and punch with holes. Arrange the oysters in a single layer on top.

Put the garlic, ginger and spring onion in a bowl, mix together well, then sprinkle over the oysters. Spoon 1 teaspoon of soy sauce over each oyster and cover the steamer with a lid. Sit the steamer over a wok or saucepan of simmering water and steam for about 2 minutes.

Heat the peanut oil in a small saucepan until smoking and carefully drizzle a little over each oyster. Garnish with the coriander leaves and serve immediately.

prawns in banana leaves

serves 4

2.5 cm (1 inch) piece **ginger**, grated

2 small **red chillies**, seeded and finely chopped

4 **spring onions (scallions)**, finely chopped

2 **lemon grass stems**, white part only, finely chopped

2 teaspoons grated **palm sugar** or **soft brown sugar**

1 tablespoon **fish sauce**

2 tablespoons **lime juice**

1 tablespoon **sesame seeds**, toasted

2 tablespoons chopped **coriander (cilantro) leaves**

1 kg (2 lb 4 oz) **raw prawns (shrimp)**, peeled and deveined

8 small **banana leaves** (see tip)

boiling **water**, for soaking

Put the ginger, chilli, spring onion and lemon grass in a food processor and pulse in short bursts until a paste forms (alternatively, you can do this in a mortar and pestle). Transfer the paste to a bowl, then stir in the sugar, fish sauce, lime juice, sesame seeds and coriander and mix well. Add the prawns and toss to coat. Cover and marinate in the refrigerator for 2 hours.

Meanwhile, put the banana leaves in a large heatproof bowl, cover with boiling water and leave them to soak for 3 minutes, or until softened. Drain and pat dry. Cut the banana leaves into 18 cm (7 inch) squares.

Divide the prawn mixture into eight, and place one portion on each square of banana leaf. Fold the leaf to enclose the mixture, and then secure the parcels with a wooden skewer. Put the parcels in a steamer and cover with a lid. Sit the steamer over a wok or saucepan of boiling water and steam for 8–10 minutes, or until the filling is cooked.

tip **Banana leaves are used throughout Asia to wrap foods for steaming or baking. They keep the food moist and impart a mild flavour. Buy them from Asian food stores if you don't have access to fresh leaves.**

zucchini flowers stuffed with moroccan spiced chickpeas

serves 4

150 g (5 1/2 oz) **butternut pumpkin (squash)**, chopped

300 g (10 1/2 oz) tin **chickpeas**, drained and rinsed

2 tablespoons **currants**

4 **red Asian shallots**, finely chopped

1/2 teaspoon **ground cumin**

1/2 teaspoon **ground cinnamon**

1 1/2 tablespoons **lemon juice**

2 teaspoons chopped **coriander (cilantro) leaves**

2 teaspoons chopped **parsley**

12 large **zucchini (courgette) flowers** with stems attached

garlic and lemon butter

100 g (3 1/2 oz) **ghee** (see tip)

4 **garlic cloves**, crushed

1 teaspoon **ground coriander**

pinch of **cayenne pepper**

1 tablespoon **lemon juice**

Spoon in the pumpkin mixture, then gently twist the **flower tips** to secure the filling.

Sauté until the garlic is golden brown and the butter is **frothing**.

Place the pumpkin pieces in a steamer and cover with a lid. Sit the steamer over a saucepan or wok of boiling water and steam for 5–8 minutes, or until the pumpkin is soft. Transfer the pumpkin to a bowl, allow to cool then mash well with a fork.

Meanwhile, coarsely mash the chickpeas in a separate bowl. Add the currants, shallots, cumin, cinnamon, lemon juice, coriander and parsley and season with salt and freshly ground black pepper. Fold the mashed pumpkin through the mixture until well combined.

Carefully remove the stamens from inside the zucchini flowers and trim the ends. Fill each flower until almost full, then gently twist the flower tips to secure the filling. Lay the stuffed flowers in the steamer so they all fit snugly in a single layer.

Sit the steamer over a saucepan or wok of boiling water and steam for 5–8 minutes, or until the zucchini stems are just tender when tested.

Meanwhile, to make the garlic and lemon butter, melt the ghee in a small saucepan over medium heat. Add the garlic and 1/2 teaspoon of salt and sauté for 2 minutes, or until the garlic starts to turn golden brown and the butter is frothing. Add the coriander and cayenne pepper and cook 30 seconds. Stir in the lemon juice.

Put three stuffed zucchini flowers on each plate and drizzle with some of the hot garlic and lemon butter.

tip **Ghee is clarified butter, or pure butter fat. It can be heated to higher temperatures than regular butter without burning. It is available in small tins or bars in most supermarkets.**

pork and prawn dumplings

makes 24

300 g ($10\frac{1}{2}$ oz) **minced (ground) pork**

300 g ($10\frac{1}{2}$ oz) **minced (ground) prawns (shrimp)**

3 **spring onions (scallions)**, finely sliced

60 g ($2\frac{1}{4}$ oz/$\frac{1}{3}$ cup) chopped **water chestnuts**

$1\frac{1}{2}$ teaspoons finely chopped fresh **ginger**

1 tablespoon **light soy sauce**, plus extra, to serve

1 teaspoon **caster (superfine) sugar**

24 **won ton wrappers**

chilli sauce, to serve

To make the filling, put the pork and prawn meat, spring onion, water chestnuts, ginger, soy sauce and sugar in a large non-metallic bowl and combine well.

Working with one wrapper at a time, place a heaped tablespoon of filling in the centre of the wrapper. Bring the sides up around the outside, forming pleats to firmly encase the filling — the top of the dumpling should be exposed. Pinch together to enclose the bottom of the filling, then cover with a damp cloth. Repeat with the remaining wrappers and filling to make 24 in total.

Line a large steamer with baking paper and punch with holes. Place the dumplings on top in a single layer, making sure they don't touch one another. Cover with a lid. Sit the steamer over a wok or saucepan of boiling water and steam for 8–10 minutes, or until cooked through. Serve the dumplings with the soy and chilli sauces, for dipping.

tip **If you prefer, these dumplings can be made without the prawns — just double the amount of pork.**

chicken and coconut rice in banana leaves

makes about 12

2–3 young **banana leaves**, or foil

400 g (14 oz/2 cups) **glutinous white rice**

185 ml (6 fl oz/3/4 cup) **coconut milk**

chicken filling

2 tablespoons **oil**

2–3 **garlic cloves**, crushed

6 **curry leaves** (see tip)

1 teaspoon **dried shrimp paste**

2 teaspoons **ground coriander**

2 teaspoons **ground cumin**

1/2 teaspoon **ground turmeric**

250 g (9 oz) **minced (ground) chicken**

3 tablespoons **coconut milk**

1 teaspoon **lemon juice**

With a sharp knife, cut away the central ribs of the banana leaves. The leaves will split into large pieces — cut these into 15 cm (6 inch) squares. Blanch in boiling water briefly to soften them, then spread out on a tea towel (dish cloth) and cover.

Wash and drain the rice, then put it in a large heavy-based saucepan with 435 ml (15 1/4 fl oz/1 3/4 cups) of water. Bring slowly to the boil, then reduce the heat to very low, cover tightly and cook for 15 minutes.

Put the coconut milk and 125 ml (4 fl oz/1/2 cup) of water in a small saucepan and heat without boiling. Pour over the rice and stir through with a fork. Transfer to a bowl and set aside to cool.

To make the chicken filling, heat the oil in a large heavy-based frying pan over medium heat, add the garlic and curry leaves and stir for 1 minute. Add the dried shrimp paste, coriander, cumin and turmeric and cook for another minute. Add the chicken and cook, breaking up with a fork, for 3–4 minutes, or until the chicken changes colour. Pour in the coconut milk and cook over low heat for 5 minutes, or until absorbed. Remove the curry leaves. Add the lemon juice and season with salt and pepper, to taste. Leave to cool.

Place 1 heaped tablespoon of rice in the centre of each piece of banana leaf and flatten to a 4 cm (1 1/2 inch) square. Top with a heaped teaspoon of filling. Roll the leaf into a parcel and place, seam side down, in a steamer lined with leftover banana leaf scraps (you may have to do this in batches). Cover with a lid, sit the steamer over a wok or saucepan of boiling water and steam for 15 minutes. Serve at room temperature with chopsticks or small forks.

tip **Curry leaves can be bought fresh or dried from Asian food stores. They have a distinctive flavour and cannot be substituted.**

Pour the hot **coconut milk** over the rice and stir through with a fork.

Put the rice and filling on a piece of **banana leaf** and roll the leaf into a parcel.

pearl balls

makes 15–18 balls

1 small **dried shiitake mushroom**

300 g (10½ oz) **minced (ground) pork**

150 g (5½ oz) **raw prawns (shrimp)**, peeled, deveined and roughly chopped

1 tablespoon chopped **spring onion (scallion)**

2 teaspoons finely chopped fresh **ginger**

2 teaspoons finely chopped **lemon grass**, white part only

1 **makrut (kaffir lime) leaf**, finely shredded

1 **garlic clove**, finely chopped

1 teaspoon **fish sauce**

1 **egg**

1 tablespoon chopped **coriander (cilantro) leaves**

200 g (7 oz/1 cup) **glutinous white rice**

sweet chilli sauce, to serve

Soak the mushroom in hot water for 20 minutes. Remove the stalk and finely chop the cap.

Combine the pork and prawn meat, spring onion, ginger, lemon grass, lime leaf, garlic, fish sauce and egg in a food processor. Pulse for 10–15 seconds, or until combined, then transfer to a bowl and stir in the mushroom and coriander.

Put the rice in a bowl. With wet hands, roll the pork mixture into balls about 2.5 cm (1 inch) in diameter. Gently roll each ball in the rice until they are evenly covered.

Line a double steamer with baking paper and punch with holes. Place the balls in the steamer and cover with a lid. Sit the steamer over a wok or saucepan of boiling water and steam for 1 hour–1 hour 15 minutes, or until the rice is cooked, replenishing the water when necessary. Serve with sweet chilli sauce.

vegetable dumplings

makes 25

1 tablespoon **oil**
3 **spring onions (scallions)**, sliced
2 **garlic cloves**, chopped
2 teaspoons grated fresh **ginger**
3 tablespoons snipped **garlic chives**
425 g (15 oz/1 bunch) **choy sum**, shredded
2 tablespoons **sweet chilli sauce**
3 tablespoons chopped **coriander (cilantro) leaves**
40 g (1 1/2 oz/1/4 cup) tinned **water chestnuts**, drained and chopped
25 **round gow gee dumpling wrappers**

dipping sauce

1/2 teaspoon **sesame oil**
1/2 teaspoon **peanut oil**
1 tablespoon **soy sauce**
1 tablespoon **lime juice**
1 small **red chilli**, seeded and finely chopped

Heat the oil in a frying pan over medium heat and cook the spring onion, garlic, ginger and chives for 1–2 minutes, or until soft. Increase the heat to high, add the choy sum and cook for 4–5 minutes, or until wilted. Stir in the chilli sauce, coriander and water chestnuts. Allow to cool. If the mixture is too wet, squeeze dry.

Lay a wrapper on the work surface. Place a heaped teaspoon of the filling in the centre. Moisten the edge of the wrapper with water and pinch to seal, forming a ball. Repeat with the remaining wrappers and filling to make 25 dumplings.

Line a steamer with baking paper and punch with holes. Arrange the dumplings, seam side up, in the steamer in a single layer and cover with a lid. Sit the steamer over a wok or saucepan of boiling water and steam for 5–6 minutes, or until the dumpling wrappers have softened and the filling is cooked.

Meanwhile, to make the dipping sauce, combine all the ingredients in a small bowl. Serve with the dumplings.

zucchini stuffed with pork and prawns

makes about 24

4 large **zucchini (courgettes)**

125 g (4 1/2 oz) **minced (ground) pork**

60 g (2 1/4 oz) **raw prawns (shrimp)**, peeled, deveined and finely chopped

2 **garlic cloves**, crushed

2 tablespoons finely chopped **coriander (cilantro) leaves**

1/2 teaspoon **sugar**

2 **makrut (kaffir lime) leaves**, finely chopped, or 1 teaspoon grated **lime zest**

2 **red Asian shallots**, finely chopped

2 teaspoons **fish sauce**

3 tablespoons **coconut cream**

1 tablespoon toasted **unsalted peanuts**, finely chopped

Cut the zucchini into 4 cm (1 1/2 inch) thick slices. Scoop out the centre with a melon baller, leaving 5 mm (1/4 inch) of flesh around the inside of the skin as well as on the bottom of each slice.

In a small bowl, combine the pork, prawn meat, garlic, coriander, sugar, lime leaves, shallots, fish sauce and 2 tablespoons of the coconut cream. Spoon the mixture into the zucchini shells.

Arrange the zucchini shells in a single layer in a steamer and cover with a lid. Sit the steamer over a wok or saucepan of boiling water and steam for 10 minutes, or until the filling is cooked and the zucchini is tender. Drizzle with the remaining coconut cream and sprinkle the chopped peanuts over the top.

stuffed shiitake

serves 4–6

stuffing

300 g (10 1/2 oz) **raw prawns (shrimp)**, peeled, deveined and finely chopped
150 g (5 1/2 oz) **minced (ground) chicken**
50 g (1 3/4 oz) **pork rind**, very finely chopped (ask your butcher for this)
30 g (1 oz) **ham**, finely chopped
1 **spring onion (scallion)**, finely chopped
2 large **garlic cloves**, crushed
1 1/2 tablespoons finely chopped **water chestnuts**
1 1/2 tablespoons finely chopped **bamboo shoots**
1 1/2 teaspoons grated fresh **ginger**
1 tablespoon **Chinese rice wine**
1 tablespoon **oyster sauce**
1 tablespoon **light soy sauce**
2–3 drops of **sesame oil**
1 **egg white**, beaten until frothy
1/4 teaspoon **sugar**
pinch of **Chinese five-spice**
white pepper, to taste

300 g (10 1/2 oz) **shiitake mushrooms** (see tip)
1 litre (35 fl oz/4 cups) **chicken stock**
1 **star anise**
oyster sauce, to serve
toasted **sesame seeds**, to garnish (optional)

Put all the stuffing **ingredients** in a large bowl and **mix** together thoroughly.

Generously fill each mushroom cap with stuffing, then round the **tops**.

To make the stuffing, put the prawns, chicken, pork rind, ham, spring onion, garlic, water chestnuts, bamboo shoots, ginger, rice wine, oyster sauce, soy sauce, sesame oil, egg white, sugar, five-spice and white pepper in a bowl and mix together thoroughly.

Remove the stalks from the shiitake and reserve. Generously fill each mushroom cap with stuffing, rounding the tops slightly. The amount of stuffing you use for each mushroom will differ depending on their size — if the mushrooms are very small you may have some mixture left over.

Pour the chicken stock and 500 ml (17 fl oz/2 cups) of water into a wok and add the star anise and reserved mushroom stalks. Bring to the boil over high heat, then reduce the heat and keep at a slow boil.

Line a large steamer with baking paper and punch with holes. Place the mushrooms in a single layer on top, filling side up. Cover with a lid, sit the steamer over the boiling stock mixture and steam for 15 minutes, or until the filling and the mushrooms are cooked through. Place on a serving platter and pour on a little of the stock. Drizzle with a little oyster sauce and garnish with the sesame seeds.

tip **When purchasing fresh shiitake, choose mushrooms that are plump, with firm caps that curl under. Avoid those with shrivelled, dehydrated caps as they are well past their peak. Choose mushrooms of a similar size so they cook evenly.**

clams with corn and bacon

serves 4

25 g (1 oz) **butter**

1 large **onion**, chopped

100 g (3 1/2 oz) **bacon**, chopped

1.5 kg (3 lb 5 oz) fresh **clams (vongole)**, cleaned (see tip)

1 large **corn cob**, kernels removed

150 ml (5 fl oz) **dry alcoholic cider**

3 tablespoons **fish stock**

150 ml (5 fl oz) **thick (double/heavy) cream**

Melt the butter in a large saucepan over medium heat. Add the onion and bacon and cook for 5 minutes, or until the onion is soft and the bacon is cooked.

Arrange the clams in a single layer in a steamer and cover with a lid. Sit the steamer over a saucepan or wok of boiling water and steam for 8–10 minutes, or until the clams start to open. Discard any clams that have not opened.

Add the corn kernels to the onion and bacon and cook, stirring, for 3–4 minutes, or until tender. Pour in the cider and fish stock, bring to the boil, then reduce the heat and simmer for 2 minutes. Stir in the cream, and season with salt and freshly ground black pepper. Tip in the clams and toss them gently in the sauce. Serve in warmed deep bowls.

tip **If clams are unavailable, this recipe works just as well with pipis, cockles or mussels.**

salads

salmon and pasta salad

serves 4

500 g (1 lb 2 oz) **salmon steaks**
2 tablespoons **lemon juice**
300 g (10 1/2 oz) **penne**
3 tablespoons **red wine vinegar**
1 tablespoon **dijon mustard**
125 ml (4 fl oz/1/2 cup) **olive oil**
80 g (2 3/4 oz/1/2 cup) **pine nuts**, toasted
200 g (7 oz/heaped 3/4 cup) **ricotta cheese**, crumbled
1 handful **basil**, roughly chopped
4 tablespoons roughly chopped **flat-leaf (Italian) parsley**
35 g (1 1/4 oz/1/3 cup) coarsely grated **parmesan cheese**
80 g (2 3/4 oz/1 3/4 cups) **baby rocket (arugula)**
200 g (7 oz) **cherry tomatoes**, halved

Line a steamer with baking paper and punch with holes. Place the salmon steaks on top and cover with a lid. Sit the steamer over a saucepan or wok of boiling water and steam for 5 minutes, or until just cooked (they should still be a little pink in the centre). Remove from the steamer. When the steaks are cool enough to handle, remove the skin and bones and break the flesh into chunks. Drizzle with lemon juice and season with salt and freshly ground black pepper.

Cook the penne according to the packet instructions, then drain and leave to cool.

To make a quick dressing, put the vinegar and mustard in a small jar and shake well. Add the oil and shake until combined.

Put the salmon, penne, pine nuts, ricotta, basil, parsley, parmesan, rocket and tomatoes in a large bowl, drizzle with the dressing and toss gently to combine.

vietnamese pork and rice vermicelli salad

serves 4

1 **lemon grass stem**, white part only, roughly chopped
2 **garlic cloves**, peeled
4 cm (1 1/2 inch) piece **ginger**, roughly chopped
1 large **red chilli**, seeded and roughly chopped
500 g (1 lb 2 oz) **minced (ground) pork**
200 g (7 oz) **dried rice vermicelli**
boiling **water**, for soaking
50 g (1 3/4 oz/1/3 cup) toasted **peanuts**, chopped
250 g (9 oz) **baby roma (plum) tomatoes**, halved
4 **spring onions (scallions)**, finely sliced (including most of the green stem)
1 **Lebanese (short) cucumber**, halved lengthways and finely sliced
1 large handful **coriander (cilantro) leaves**
1 very large handful **mint**, torn

dressing

4 tablespoons **lime juice**
3 tablespoons **fish sauce**
2 large **red chillies**, seeded and finely chopped
1 tablespoon grated **palm sugar** or **soft brown sugar**
4 tablespoons **kecap manis** (see tip)

Scatter the pork mixture evenly over the **base** of the steamer.

Drain the **vermicelli**, then cut the long strands in half with a pair of **scissors**.

Put the lemon grass, garlic, ginger and chilli in a food processor and pulse until finely chopped. Empty the mixture into a large bowl and add the minced pork and 1 teaspoon of salt. Use clean hands to mix until well combined.

Line the base of a large steamer with baking paper and punch with holes. Carefully scatter the pork mixture over the base of the steamer and cover with a lid. Sit the steamer over a wok or saucepan of boiling water and steam for 5 minutes, or until cooked through. Stir occasionally with a fork to break up any of the lumps. Remove from the heat and set aside to cool a little (it should still be warm).

Put the vermicelli in a large bowl and pour in enough boiling to cover. Leave to soak for 10 minutes, or until translucent and softened.

Meanwhile, to make the dressing, combine the lime juice, fish sauce, chilli, sugar, kecap manis and 2 tablespoons of water in a bowl. Stir until the sugar has dissolved.

Drain the vermicelli into a colander and rinse with cold water. Drain well. Using scissors, cut the long strands in half then tip the noodles into a large bowl. Pour the dressing over the top and leave for 10 minutes. Add the pork, then stir in the remaining ingredients and toss well.

tip **If you don't have any kecap manis, soy sauce mixed with a little soft brown sugar can be substituted.**

puy lentil salad with tomatoes and rocket

serves 4

200 g (7 oz/1 cup) **puy lentils** or tiny **blue-green lentils**
boiling **water**, for soaking
3 ripe **tomatoes**, finely chopped
1/2 small **red onion**, finely chopped
40 g (1 1/2 oz/1/3 cup) chopped **walnuts** or **pecans**, lightly toasted
4 tablespoons finely chopped **parsley**
1 tablespoon **thyme**
60 g (2 1/4 oz) **goat's cheese**, crumbled
175 g (6 oz/1 bunch) **asparagus**, trimmed and halved on the diagonal
100 g (3 1/2 oz/4 cups) **baby rocket (arugula)**

dressing

2 tablespoons **olive oil**
2 tablespoons **balsamic vinegar**
2 teaspoons **dijon mustard**
1 teaspoon **honey**

Put the lentils in a bowl and cover with boiling water. Soak for 30 minutes then drain. Line a steamer with baking paper and punch with holes. Put the lentils in the steamer and cover with a lid. Sit the steamer over a saucepan of boiling water and steam for 30 minutes, or until the lentils are tender. Refresh under cold water and put in a large bowl.

Add the tomato, onion, walnuts, parsley and thyme to the lentils. Combine the dressing ingredients and toss through the salad. Gently fold in the goat's cheese.

Put the asparagus in a steamer in a single layer and cover with a lid. Sit the steamer over a saucepan of boiling water and steam for 2–3 minutes, or until just tender.

Divide the rocket leaves among serving plates. Spoon on the lentil salad and arrange the asparagus on top.

tip **Replace the goat's cheese with soft feta and the rocket with mixed salad leaves if preferred.**

lime and prawn salad

serves 4

16 large **raw prawns (shrimp)**, peeled and deveined, tails intact
200 g (7 oz) **baby green beans**
2 **Lebanese (short) cucumbers**, sliced
4 **spring onions (scallions)**, finely chopped
1 tablespoon finely shredded **makrut (kaffir lime) leaves** (see tip)
15 g (1/2 oz/1/4 cup) **flaked coconut**
2 teaspoons shredded **lime zest**

dressing

1 tablespoon **peanut oil**
1 tablespoon **fish sauce**
1 tablespoon grated **palm sugar** or **soft brown sugar**
1 tablespoon chopped **coriander (cilantro) leaves**
2 teaspoons **soy sauce**
1–2 teaspoons **sweet chilli sauce**
3 tablespoons **lime juice**

Put the prawns and beans in a steamer and cover with a lid. Sit the steamer over a wok or saucepan of boiling water and steam for 6 minutes. Remove from the steamer and refresh the beans in cold water. Drain and pat dry with paper towels.

To make the dressing, whisk together all the ingredients in a bowl.

Combine the prawns, beans, cucumber, spring onion, lime leaves and flaked coconut in a large bowl. Add the dressing and toss gently to coat. Transfer the salad to a large serving bowl and garnish with the shredded lime zest.

tip **Young lemon leaves can be used in place of the makrut (kaffir lime) leaves if they are not available.**

bean and vegetable salad with chilli and black vinegar dressing

serves 4

2 **fennel bulbs**, trimmed and sliced lengthways
125 g (4 1/2 oz/2/3 cup) **baby corn**, halved on the diagonal
150 g (5 1/2 oz) **snow peas (mangetout)**, trimmed and halved on the diagonal
400 g (14 oz) tin **pinto** or **borlotti (cranberry) beans**, drained and rinsed
100 g (3 1/2 oz/4 cups) **baby rocket (arugula)**
40 g (1 1/2 oz/1 heaped cup) **snow pea (mangetout) sprouts**

black vinegar dressing
4 tablespoons **olive oil**
3 tablespoons **black vinegar** (see tip)
1 tablespoon **rice vinegar**
2 tablespoons finely chopped **coriander (cilantro) leaves**
1 small **red chilli**, seeded and finely chopped

Line a steamer with baking paper and punch with holes. Put the fennel and baby corn in the steamer and cover with a lid. Sit the steamer over a saucepan or wok of boiling water and steam for 5 minutes. Add the snow peas and beans and steam for a further 5 minutes. Transfer to a bowl, making sure you leave any condensed steaming liquid on the baking paper.

Meanwhile, to make the dressing, whisk together the oil, black vinegar and rice vinegar until well combined. Season well. Stir in the coriander and chilli.

Pour half the dressing over the vegetables, toss well, then leave for 5 minutes or to cool completely. Arrange the rocket leaves on a serving platter and drizzle with the remaining dressing. Spoon on the dressed vegetables and scatter the snow pea sprouts over the top.

tip **Black vinegar is similar to balsamic, but has a slightly smoky flavour. Buy it from Asian food stores or in the Asian section of larger supermarkets.**

sake-steamed chicken salad

serves 4

250 ml (9 fl oz/1 cup) **cooking sake** (see tip)
100 ml (3 1/2 fl oz) **chicken** or **vegetable stock**
5 cm (2 inch) piece **ginger**, grated
2 **garlic cloves**, crushed
6 **coriander (cilantro) roots**, washed well
4 **black peppercorns**, cracked
2 **bay leaves**
600 g (1 lb 5 oz) boneless, skinless **chicken breast**, cut into thin strips
75 g (2 1/2 oz) **watercress**, trimmed, or 100 g (3 1/2 oz) other **salad leaves**
3 **spring onions (scallions)**, sliced

coriander dressing

4 tablespoons **olive oil**
1 tablespoon **red** or **white wine vinegar**
2 tablespoons chopped **coriander (cilantro) leaves**
2 tablespoons chopped **flat-leaf (Italian) parsley**

Combine the sake, stock, ginger, garlic, coriander roots, peppercorns and bay leaves in a jug. Put the chicken strips in a heatproof shallow dish that fits into a large steamer and pour the sauce over the chicken. Toss to mix well.

Put the dish in the steamer and cover with a lid. Sit the steamer over a wok or saucepan of boiling water and steam for 20–25 minutes, or until the chicken is cooked through, turning the chicken a couple of times during cooking to prevent it all sticking together. Remove the chicken from the liquid, reserving the liquid.

Meanwhile, to make the dressing, combine the oil and vinegar with 3 tablespoons of the cooking liquid and whisk well to combine. Add the coriander and parsley and season with salt and freshly ground black pepper. Spoon half of the dressing over the chicken, mix well, then leave to cool.

Put the chicken and watercress in a bowl, drizzle with the remaining dressing and scatter the spring onion over the top.

tip **Cooking sake is less expensive than regular sake and is available from Asian food stores or the Asian section of larger supermarkets.**

octopus, artichoke and feta salad

serves 4

800 g (1 lb 12 oz) **baby octopus**, cleaned (see tip)
3 teaspoons **oregano**, finely chopped
2 **garlic cloves**, finely chopped
1 **long red chilli**, seeded and finely chopped
3 teaspoons **lime zest**
4 tablespoons **lime juice**
3 tablespoons **extra virgin olive oil**
100 g (3 1/2 oz) **baby green beans**, trimmed
125 g (4 1/2 oz/5 cups) **baby rocket (arugula)**
1 handful **mint**, leaves torn if large
250 g (9 oz) **marinated artichoke hearts**, drained and halved
120 g (4 1/4 oz) **marinated feta cheese**, roughly crumbled
1 1/2 tablespoons **baby salted capers**, rinsed and squeezed dry

In a non-metallic bowl, combine the octopus, oregano, garlic, chilli, lime zest, 2 tablespoons of lime juice and 2 tablespoons of oil. Season well, then cover with plastic wrap and marinate in the refrigerator for 30 minutes.

Line a steamer with baking paper and punch with holes. Place the octopus and beans on top in a single layer and cover with a lid. Sit the steamer over a saucepan or wok of boiling water and steam for 5 minutes, or until cooked through. Allow to cool for 5 minutes, reserving the cooking juices.

Scatter the rocket and mint leaves on a serving dish, then add the artichoke, feta, capers, beans and octopus. Combine the remaining lime juice, oil and 1 tablespoon of the cooking juices. Drizzle over the salad, toss gently, then season and serve.

tip **Ask your fishmonger to clean the octopus for you.**

chicken and green bean salad

serves 4–6

400 g (14 oz) **minced (ground) chicken**
1 **onion**, finely chopped
3 **garlic cloves**, finely chopped
2 **lemon grass stems**, white part only, finely chopped
2 **makrut (kaffir lime) leaves**, finely chopped
1 small **red chilli**, seeded and finely chopped
2 tablespoons **peanut oil**
1 tablespoon grated **palm sugar** or **soft brown sugar**
1 teaspoon **ground turmeric**

salad

500 g (1 lb 2 oz) **green beans**, trimmed and cut into 1 cm (1/2 inch) lengths
30 g (1 oz/1/2 cup) **shredded coconut**, toasted
4 **garlic cloves**, sliced
4 **red Asian shallots**, halved and finely sliced
2 large **red chillies**, seeded and cut into thin strips
1 **makrut (kaffir lime) leaf**, finely shredded
1 large handful **coriander (cilantro) leaves**
2 tablespoons **peanut oil**
2 teaspoons **sesame oil**
juice of 2 **limes**
2 teaspoons grated **palm sugar** or **soft brown sugar**
1–2 tablespoons **fish sauce**

Put the chicken, onion, garlic, lemon grass, lime leaves, chilli, oil, sugar and turmeric in a large bowl. Mix well to combine and season with salt and pepper. Lay a piece of foil on a flat surface and top with a sheet of baking paper. Place half the chicken mixture lengthways in the centre and roll up tightly to form a log shape. Repeat with the remaining mixture to make two logs.

Place the parcels in a single layer in a steamer and cover with a lid. Sit the steamer over a wok or saucepan of boiling water and steam for 20–25 minutes, or until the chicken is cooked through. Remove the parcels from the steamer and set aside to cool slightly.

To make the salad, place the beans in the same steamer and steam for 5 minutes. Refresh under cold water. Combine the coconut, garlic, shallots, chilli, lime leaf and coriander in a salad bowl. Unwrap the chicken and break up with a fork to its original minced form. Stir the chicken and beans through the salad mixture.

Combine the peanut and sesame oils, lime juice, sugar and fish sauce in a jug. Pour the dressing over the salad and toss to combine.

tip **You can use minced (ground) beef or pork instead of chicken, if you prefer.**

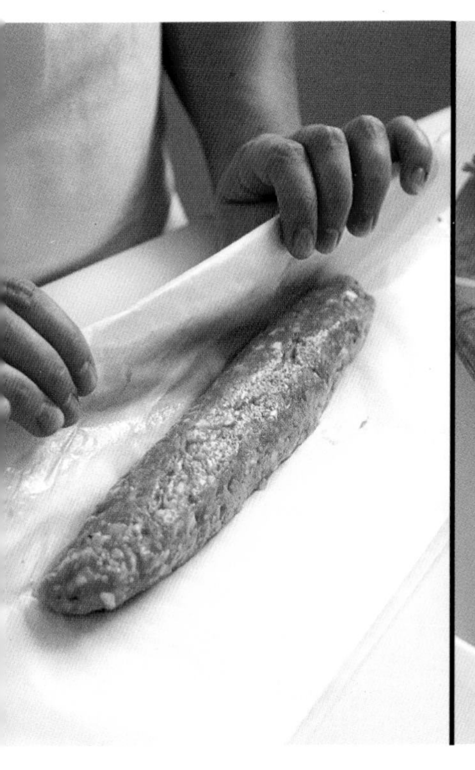

Put half of the chicken mixture **lengthways** on the baking paper and roll up to form a **log**.

Combine the coconut, garlic, shallots, chilli, lime leaf and coriander in a bowl.

potato, spinach, white bean and avocado salad

serves 4–6

6 **desiree** or other **all-purpose potatoes**, washed
2 **red capsicums (peppers)**, halved and seeded
100 g (3 1/2 oz) **snow peas (mangetout)**, trimmed
3 tablespoons **extra virgin olive oil**
2 **garlic cloves**, finely chopped
1 teaspoon **fish sauce**
1 teaspoon grated **palm sugar** or **soft brown sugar**
125 ml (4 fl oz/1/2 cup) **lime juice**
400 g (14 oz) tin **cannellini beans**, drained and rinsed
50 g (1 3/4 oz/1 cup) **baby English spinach**
1 large handful **coriander (cilantro) leaves**
2 **avocados**, diced
1 **French shallot**, finely chopped
1 small **red chilli**, seeded and finely chopped

Line a double steamer with baking paper and punch with holes. Lay the potatoes in the bottom tray and the capsicum in the top. Cover with a lid. Sit the steamer over a saucepan or wok of boiling water and steam for 30 minutes, or until the potatoes are tender. Put the capsicum in a plastic bag to cool, then peel and slice into strips.

Lightly steam the snow peas for 1–2 minutes, then slice into strips.

Meanwhile, peel the potatoes while they are still hot and cut into 1 cm (1/2 inch) rounds. Combine the oil, garlic, fish sauce, sugar and 3 tablespoons of the lime juice in a jug. Put the potato rounds in a bowl and pour on half the dressing.

Put the capsicum, snow peas, cannellini beans, spinach and coriander in a large bowl. Pour on the remaining dressing and toss to combine. In a separate bowl combine the avocado, shallot, chilli and remaining lime juice.

To serve, divide the potato slices among serving plates. Pile the bean salad over the potatoes and top with a good dollop of the avocado mixture.

multicoloured salad

serves 6

6 **baby beetroot (beets)**

200 g (7 oz/1 bunch) **broccolini**, cut into 4 cm (1 1/2 inch) lengths

6 **new potatoes**

6 **red coral lettuce leaves**, torn

1 roasted **red capsicum (pepper)**, cut into 1 cm (1/2 inch) strips (see tip)

1 roasted **yellow capsicum (pepper)**, cut into 1 cm (1/2 inch) strips (see tip)

125 g (4 1/2 oz) **yellow teardrop tomatoes**, halved

125 g (4 1/2 oz) **cherry tomatoes**, halved

1/2 **red onion**, finely sliced

1 tablespoon chopped **tarragon**

3 tablespoons **extra virgin olive oil**

2 tablespoons **balsamic vinegar**

1/2 teaspoon **wholegrain mustard**

Wrap each beetroot in foil and place in a steamer with the broccolini and potatoes. Cover and sit the steamer over a saucepan or wok of boiling water. Remove the broccolini after 2–3 minutes, or when just cooked, the potatoes after about 20 minutes, or when easily pierced with a skewer, and the beetroot after 40 minutes, or when easily pierced (replenish the water if necessary). Allow the vegetables to cool then remove the skin from the beetroot and potatoes and cut into quarters.

Arrange the lettuce on a platter and top with the beetroot, broccolini, potato, red and yellow capsicum, tomatoes, onion and tarragon.

Combine the oil, vinegar and mustard in a screw-top jar and season with salt and pepper. Shake well, then pour the dressing over the salad.

tip **To roast capsicums, cut them into large flattish pieces and remove the membrane and seeds. Cook, skin side up, under a hot grill (broiler) until the skin blackens and blisters. Cool in a plastic bag, then peel and slice.**

cuttlefish and fennel salad

serves 4

750 g (1 lb 10 oz) **cuttlefish** or **squid**, cleaned and cut into thin strips
1 small **fennel bulb**, finely sliced, reserving the fronds
1/2 **red onion**, finely sliced
80 g (2 3/4 oz/3 cups) **rocket (arugula)**

dressing

2 tablespoons **lime juice**
1 tablespoon **sherry vinegar**
1 **garlic clove**, crushed
1/4 teaspoon **chilli flakes**
3 tablespoons **extra virgin olive oil**
1 tablespoon **wholegrain mustard**

Place the cuttlefish on a plate in a steamer and cover with a lid. Sit the steamer over a saucepan or wok of boiling water and steam for about 3 minutes, or until just cooked. Cool, then place in a bowl with the fennel, onion and 2 tablespoons of the finely chopped fennel fronds.

Mix all the dressing ingredients together in a bowl or a screw-top jar and pour over the salad. Toss gently and season to taste.

Arrange the rocket leaves on a serving plate and top with the salad.

sweet potato, squash and spinach salad

serves 4

800 g (1 lb 12 oz) **orange sweet potato**, cut into 1 cm (1/2 inch) thick rounds, then halved or quartered
350 g (12 oz) **baby (pattypan) squash**, sliced lengthways into 4 pieces
150 g (51/2 oz/3 cups) **baby English spinach**
60 g (21/4 oz/1/2 cup) **slivered almonds**, toasted
6 **bulb spring onions (scallions)**, finely sliced (including some of the green part)
1 large handful **coriander (cilantro) leaves**

dressing

1/4 **preserved lemon**, flesh and pith removed, zest finely chopped
2 teaspoons **honey**
1 **garlic clove**, finely chopped
1/2 teaspoon **ground cumin**
1/2 teaspoon **ground coriander**
2 tablespoons **apple cider vinegar**
3 tablespoons **olive oil**

Line a large steamer with baking paper and punch with holes. Put the sweet potato on top and cover with a lid. Sit the steamer over a saucepan or wok of boiling water and steam for 12 minutes, or until tender. Carefully remove the potato and set aside to cool a little. Steam the squash for about 3 minutes, or until almost tender. Remove and set aside to cool a little.

Meanwhile, to make the dressing, mix together the preserved lemon, honey, garlic, cumin, coriander and vinegar in a bowl and season with salt and pepper. Pour the oil into the bowl in a steady stream and stir well to combine.

Gently combine the sweet potato, squash, spinach, almonds, spring onion and coriander in a bowl. Pour on the dressing and gently toss. Transfer to a serving platter and serve.

corn salad with asian dressing

serves 4

1 large **red capsicum (pepper)**

3 **corn cobs**, husks removed

90 g (3 1/4 oz/1 cup) **bean sprouts**, trimmed

4 **spring onions (scallions)**, finely sliced on the diagonal

asian dressing

1/2 **garlic clove**, crushed

1/2 teaspoon finely grated fresh **ginger**

1 teaspoon **sugar**

1 tablespoon **rice vinegar**

1 tablespoon **soy sauce**

1 tablespoon **lemon juice**

2 teaspoons **sesame oil**

2 tablespoons **peanut oil**

Cut the capsicum into large flattish pieces. Cook, skin side up, under a hot grill (broiler) until the skin blackens and blisters. Place in a plastic bag and leave to cool, then peel away the skin and tear the capsicum into large strips.

Using a heavy knife, slice each corn cob into six 2.5 cm (1 inch) pieces. Put the corn in a steamer and cover with a lid. Sit the steamer over a wok or saucepan of boiling water and steam for 5–8 minutes, or until tender. Arrange on a serving plate with the capsicum and bean sprouts.

To make the dressing, mix together the garlic, ginger, sugar, rice vinegar, soy sauce and lemon juice in a jug. Whisk in the oils with a fork until combined and season with pepper. Drizzle over the salad and top with spring onion.

crunchy parcel chicken salad with remoulade

serves 4

2 skinless, boneless **chicken breasts** (about 300 g/10 1/2 oz each)
1 **red onion**, finely diced
1 tablespoon roughly chopped **oregano**
1 teaspoon **dried oregano**
2 tablespoons **olive oil**

remoulade

185 g (6 1/2 oz/3/4 cup) **whole-egg mayonnaise**
2 teaspoons **dijon mustard**
1 tablespoon **capers**, rinsed and squeezed dry, chopped
25 g (1 oz) **cornichons**, finely diced
1 tablespoon finely snipped **chives**
1 **garlic clove**, crushed
1 tablespoon **lime juice**
1 tablespoon chopped **flat-leaf (Italian) parsley**

crunchy salad

2 **iceberg lettuce hearts**, shredded
2 **celery stalks**, finely sliced on the diagonal
2 **green apples**, peeled, cored and cut into thin matchsticks
4 **radishes**, trimmed and cut into thin matchsticks
100 g (3 1/2 oz/1 cup) **walnuts**, toasted and halved

Cover each breast with the **herb** mixture, then fold the baking paper over and tuck the ends **under**.

Remove the **chicken** breasts from the parcels and **finely slice** with a sharp knife.

Preheat the oven to 180°C (350°F/Gas 4). Pat dry the chicken breasts with paper towels, then place each breast on a piece of baking paper large enough to wrap the breast and its topping. Combine the onion and fresh and dried oregano in a bowl and season to taste. Lightly rub the olive oil onto each breast then cover evenly with the herb mixture. Fold the baking paper over each chicken breast, then tuck the ends underneath so it is secure. Cover each parcel with foil to help retain the juices and place in a roasting tin. Bake for about 25–30 minutes, or until cooked through. Rest for 5 minutes before opening the parcels.

Meanwhile, to make the remoulade, combine all the ingredients in a bowl and season. Cover and refrigerate until ready to serve.

Combine the salad ingredients in a bowl and toss with the remoulade.

Remove the chicken breasts from the parcels and finely slice. Arrange the slices over each plated salad and serve. This is delicious served with crusty bread.

beetroot salad

serves 4

1 tablespoon **olive oil**

50 g (1 3/4 oz/1/2 cup) **pecans**

1.3 kg (3 lb/2 bunches) **baby beetroot (beets)**, washed, trimmed and halved

250 g (9 oz) **baby green beans**, trimmed

120 g (4 1/4 oz/4 cups) **watercress**, trimmed

2 tablespoons **walnut oil**

1 teaspoon **honey**

2 teaspoons grated **orange zest**

1 tablespoon **cider vinegar**

50 g (1 3/4 oz) firm **blue cheese**, finely sliced

Heat the oil in a frying pan over medium–high heat. Add the pecans and toast for 3 minutes, then sprinkle with salt and freshly ground black pepper. Remove from the heat and pour into a bowl lined with paper towels. Drain.

Line a large steamer with baking paper and punch with holes. Put the beetroot halves on top and cover with a lid. Sit the steamer over a saucepan or wok of boiling water and steam for 30–35 minutes, or until the beetroot is tender when pierced with a knife. Remove from the steamer and allow to cool.

Remove the baking paper from the steamer and add the baby beans. Cover and steam for 5–7 minutes, or until just tender. Remove and refresh under cold water.

Peel the skins from the beetroot and trim off any excess stem. Put the pecans, beans and watercress in a large bowl and combine. Mix together the walnut oil, honey, orange zest and vinegar in a bowl, then pour over the salad. Carefully fold in the beetroot. Season to taste, then transfer to a serving platter and sprinkle the blue cheese over the top.

lemon-scented scallops with fennel and radish salad

serves 4 as a starter

1 **lemon**, sliced

400 g (14 oz) large **scallops**, roe removed

1 tablespoon grated **lemon zest**

1 **baby fennel bulb**, finely sliced (use a mandolin)

3 **radishes**, finely sliced (use a mandolin)

60 g (2 1/4 oz/2 cups) **watercress**, trimmed

1 1/2 tablespoons roughly snipped **chives**

80 g (2 3/4 oz/1/2 cup) **ligurian olives**

2 tablespoons **mayonnaise**

2 teaspoons **dijon mustard**

1 1/2 teaspoons **lemon juice**

Line a steamer with baking paper and punch with holes, then top with a layer of lemon slices. Place the scallops in a single layer on top, sprinkle with the lemon zest and cover with a lid. Sit the steamer over a saucepan or wok of simmering water and steam for 4 minutes, or until just cooked through. Allow to cool.

Combine the fennel, radish, watercress, chives and olives in a bowl.

Make a dressing by whisking together the mayonnaise, mustard and lemon juice. Season to taste.

Divide the fennel salad among four plates, top with the scallops and drizzle the dressing over the top.

squid and chickpea salad

serves 4–6

4 cleaned **squid tubes** (see tip)
100 g (3 1/2 oz/1/2 cup) **couscous**
4 tablespoons **extra virgin olive oil**
400 g (14 oz) tin **chickpeas**, drained and rinsed
3 **spring onions (scallions)**, finely sliced
2 **tomatoes**, seeded and cut into 5 mm (1/4 inch) dice
90 g (3 1/4 oz/1/2 cup) **green olives**, pitted and halved
1 large handful **parsley**, chopped
2 **garlic cloves**, crushed
3 tablespoons **lemon juice**
1 small **red chilli**, seeded and finely sliced

Cut the squid into 5 mm (1/4 inch) strips, arrange the strips in a steamer and cover with a lid. Sit the steamer over a saucepan or wok of boiling water and steam for 4 minutes, or until just cooked.

Put the couscous in a small bowl with 125 ml (4 fl oz/1/2 cup) of cold water. Leave for 5 minutes then add 1 teaspoon of the olive oil and work it through the couscous with your fingers. Line a small steamer with a clean, damp cloth — a tea towel (dish towel) is fine — tip the couscous onto the tea towel, then cover and steam over simmering water for 20 minutes. Break up any clumps gently with a fork two or three times during the cooking time. Tip the couscous into a bowl, add 1 teaspoon of olive oil and use a fork to gently separate the grains. Leave to cool.

Combine the squid, couscous, chickpeas, spring onion, tomato, olives, parsley, garlic, lemon juice, chilli and remaining oil in a large bowl, season and mix well.

tip **You can buy cleaned squid tubes from your fishmonger.**

warm greek rice salad

serves 4

20 g (3/4 oz) **butter**
1 **red onion**, finely chopped
2 **garlic cloves**, finely chopped
1 teaspoon **ground coriander**
1 teaspoon **ground cumin**
200 g (7 oz/1 cup) **basmati rice**
3 tablespoons chopped **dill**
375 ml (13 fl oz/1 1/2 cups) hot **chicken stock**
1 tablespoon **sesame seeds**, toasted
1 large handful **parsley**, roughly chopped
1 large handful **mint**, roughly chopped
4 tablespoons **lemon juice**
4 tablespoons **plain yoghurt**
100 g (3 1/2 oz/2 cups) **baby English spinach**
3 **roma (plum) tomatoes**, quartered and seeded
2 **baby fennel bulbs**, finely sliced (use a mandolin)
80 g (2 3/4 oz/1/2 cup) **ligurian olives**, pitted
2 **spring onions (scallions)**, chopped
extra virgin olive oil, to serve
lemon wedges, to serve

Heat the butter in a saucepan over medium heat and cook the onion, stirring, for about 3 minutes, or until softened. Add the garlic, coriander and cumin and cook for 1 minute, or until fragrant. Stir in the rice and dill and mix well. Season with salt and freshly ground black pepper. Add the stock, bring to the boil, then reduce the heat to low and cover the saucepan with a tight-fitting lid. Simmer for 15 minutes, or until the stock is absorbed and the rice is cooked.

Remove the pan from the heat, and stir in the sesame seeds, parsley, mint and 3 tablespoons of the lemon juice. In a separate bowl, combine the yoghurt and remaining lemon juice and season to taste.

Divide the rice among bowls and top with spinach, tomato, fennel, olives, spring onion and the yoghurt mixture. Drizzle with a little extra virgin olive oil and serve with lemon wedges, if desired. Serve immediately.

smoked trout, fennel and potato salad

serves 4–6

750 g (1 lb 10 oz) **new potatoes**

125 g (4 1/2 oz/1/2 cup) **mayonnaise**

1 1/2 tablespoons **lime juice**

1 teaspoon finely grated **lime zest**

3 tablespoons chopped **flat-leaf (Italian) parsley**

sea salt, to taste

1 tablespoon **red wine vinegar**

2 teaspoons **caster (superfine) sugar**

4 tablespoons **olive oil**

1 large **fennel bulb**, trimmed and outer skin removed

1 **red onion**, finely sliced

100 g (3 1/2 oz/4 cups) **baby rocket (arugula)**

1 tablespoon **capers**, rinsed and squeezed dry

350 g (12 oz) whole **smoked trout,** skin and bones removed, flesh shredded into bite-sized pieces

Remove the skin and bones from the **smoked trout** and shred the flesh into bite-sized pieces.

Mix together the **mayonnaise**, lime juice, lime zest and parsley.

Put the potatoes in a steamer and cover with a lid. Sit the steamer over a saucepan or wok of boiling water and steam for 20–25 minutes, or until just tender (take care not to overcook them or they will fall apart when sliced). Drain and allow to cool for 5 minutes, then cut the potatoes into 1–2 cm (1/2–3/4 inch) thick slices.

Meanwhile, combine the mayonnaise, lime juice, lime zest and parsley and season with sea salt and freshly ground black pepper.

Combine the vinegar, sugar, some sea salt and freshly ground black pepper in a large bowl and whisk until the sugar has dissolved. Slowly add the oil and continue to whisk until all the ingredients are combined. If the mixture is too thick, thin it down with 1–2 tablespoons of warm water, or until it reaches a drizzling consistency.

Add the fennel, onion, rocket and capers to the vinaigrette. Add the potatoes and half the smoked trout and toss gently to combine.

Divide the salad among serving plates and top with the remaining smoked trout. Drizzle the lime mayonnaise over each portion and serve with crusty bread.

vietnamese-style chicken and cabbage salad

serves 4

3 boneless, skinless **chicken breasts**, cut into 1 cm (1/2 inch) thick slices
1 **red chilli**, seeded and finely chopped
3 tablespoons **lime juice**
2 tablespoons grated **palm sugar** or **soft brown sugar**
3 tablespoons **fish sauce**
1/2 **Chinese cabbage**, shredded
2 **carrots**, grated
1 large handful **mint**, shredded

Line a steamer with baking paper and punch with holes. Arrange the chicken slices on top and cover with a lid. Sit the steamer over a wok or saucepan of boiling water and steam for about 10 minutes, or until cooked through. Cool, then shred into small pieces.

Meanwhile, mix together the chilli, lime juice, sugar and fish sauce.

Combine the chicken, cabbage, carrot, mint and dressing in a bowl. Toss well and serve immediately.

asparagus and orange salad

serves 4 as a starter

16 thin **asparagus** spears, trimmed

45 g (1 1/2 oz/1 1/2 cups) **watercress**, trimmed

1/2 small **red onion**, very finely sliced

1 **orange**, cut into 12 segments

1 tablespoon fresh **orange juice**

1 teaspoon finely grated **orange zest**

1 teaspoon **sugar**

1 tablespoon **red wine vinegar**

2 teaspoons **poppy seeds**

2 tablespoons **olive oil**

60 g (2 1/4 oz) soft **goat's cheese**

Place the asparagus in a steamer and cover with a lid. Sit the steamer over a saucepan or wok of rapidly boiling water and steam for 2–3 minutes, or until just tender. Rinse under cold water to cool, then combine with the watercress, red onion and orange segments on a serving dish.

Combine the orange juice, orange zest, sugar, vinegar and poppy seeds in a jug. Whisk in the oil with a fork until combined, then drizzle the dressing over the salad. Crumble the goat's cheese over the top and season to taste with salt and pepper.

mains

linguine with flaked salmon and asparagus

serves 4

2 x 200 g (7 oz) **salmon fillets**
2 teaspoons finely grated **lemon zest**
1 tablespoon **olive oil**
350 g (12 oz/2 bunches) **asparagus**, trimmed
300 g (10½ oz) **linguine**
2 tablespoons **pine nuts**, toasted
6 **bulb spring onions (scallions)**, finely chopped, including half of the green stem
150 g (5½ oz/1 bunch) **rocket (arugula)**, stems removed, leaves chopped in half

herb salsa

2 **garlic cloves**, peeled
2 **anchovy fillets**
4 tablespoons **extra virgin olive oil**
2 tablespoons **lemon juice**
1 tablespoon finely chopped **basil**
2 tablespoons finely chopped **parsley**
1 tablespoon **baby capers**, rinsed and squeezed dry

Put the salmon fillets in a large bowl. Add the lemon zest, oil and salt and pepper and massage well into the fillets. Arrange two large squares of baking paper on a clean surface and wrap up each fish fillet to make a secure parcel. Make sure you fold in the sides as you go so that no juice will escape during the steaming process. Place the wrapped fillets in a steamer and cover with a lid. Sit the steamer over a saucepan or wok of boiling water and steam for 10 minutes, or until the fish is just cooked all the way through. Remove the fish from the baking paper and pour off any juices, then set aside to cool.

Meanwhile, cut the asparagus spears into 4 cm (1 1/2 inch) lengths on the diagonal. Place the asparagus in the steamer and steam for about 3 minutes.

To make the herb salsa, crush the garlic and anchovies with a mortar and pestle. Combine the paste in a bowl with the oil and lemon juice. Stir in the basil, parsley and capers and season with freshly ground black pepper.

Cook the linguine in salted boiling water for 8–10 minutes, or until *al dente*. Drain.

Combine the pine nuts, spring onion, asparagus and linguine in a large bowl, add the salsa and and toss through gently. Carefully flake in the salmon and add the rocket leaves. Lightly toss all of the ingredients together, season to taste, then serve the pasta with an extra grind of pepper.

Wrap the fish fillets in large squares of baking paper, **folding** in the sides as you go.

Combine the pine nuts, spring onion, asparagus and **linguine** in a large bowl.

chicken with cognac and shallots

serves 4

1 tablespoon **olive oil**

30 g (1 oz) **butter**

1.8 kg (4 lb) **chicken pieces**, trimmed of excess fat

2 tablespoons **cognac** or **brandy**

8 **French shallots**, peeled

2 tablespoons **chicken stock**

2 tablespoons **dry white wine**

3 **thyme** sprigs

Heat the olive oil and half the butter in a large frying pan over medium–high heat and brown the chicken, in batches if necessary, for 6–8 minutes. Transfer the pieces to a large flameproof casserole dish with a tight-fitting lid. Put the dish over low heat, sprinkle the cognac over the chicken and flame it. To do this, light a match and lower the flame onto the cognac until it ignites, then allow the flame to extinguish itself.

Melt the remaining butter in the frying pan over medium–low heat and cook the shallots without browning for 5 minutes, or until softened. Add the chicken stock and wine, increase the heat to high and boil, stirring, for 30 seconds to deglaze the pan. Pour the contents of the pan over the chicken and add the thyme.

Cover the casserole tightly with foil and put the lid on. Cover again with foil if you feel the top isn't completely sealed. Place over very low heat, barely simmering, and cook for 45 minutes, or until tender. Transfer the chicken pieces to a plate and keep warm. Increase the heat under the casserole dish and boil until the juices thicken to a light coating consistency.

Spoon the juices over the chicken and serve immediately. For a more substantial meal, serve this with your favourite mash.

whole duck in banana leaves

serves 4

2 kg (4 lb 8 oz) **duck**

8 **red Asian shallots**, halved and sliced

6 **garlic cloves**, sliced

5 small **red chillies**, seeded and sliced

4 **makrut (kaffir lime) leaves**, finely chopped

3 **lemon grass stems**, white part only, finely chopped

2 tablespoons chopped fresh **ginger**

1 tablespoon **salt**

1 teaspoon **ground turmeric**

1 teaspoon **ground coriander**

1/2 teaspoon **ground white pepper**

3 tablespoons **peanut oil**

1 tablespoon grated **palm sugar** or **soft brown sugar**

2 teaspoons **fish sauce**

4 large **banana leaves**, to wrap

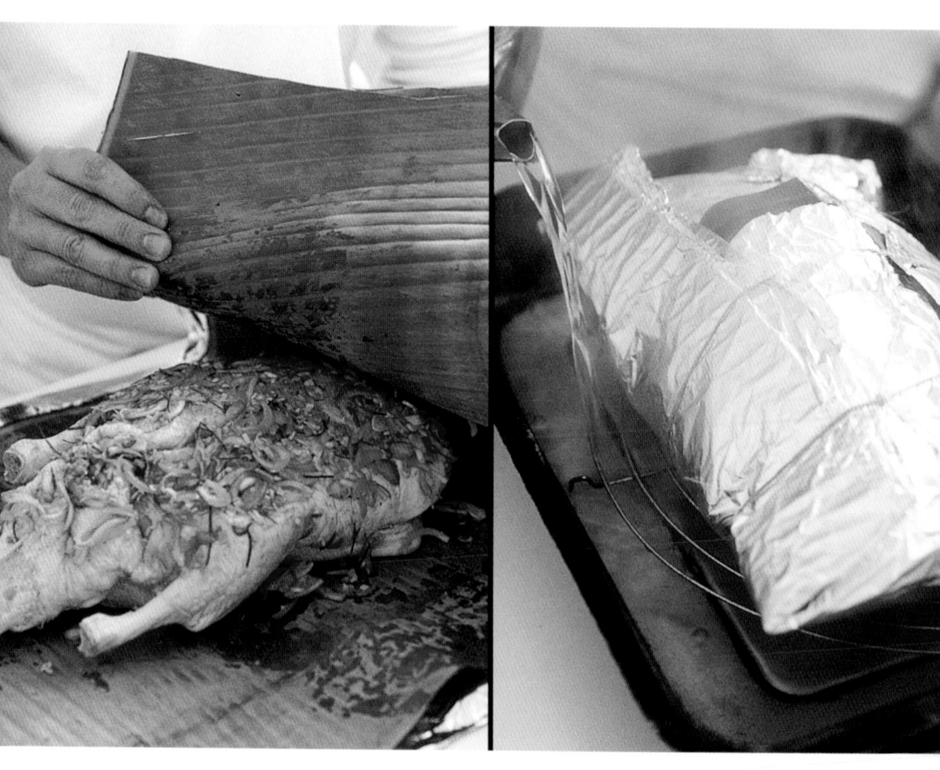

Place the **duck** on the banana leaves and wrap to completely **enclose**.

Lay the duck on a **rack** in a large roasting tin and pour in enough **hot water** to come halfway up the sides.

Preheat the oven to 180°C (350°F/Gas 4). Wash the duck inside and out and pat dry with paper towels. Combine all the remaining ingredients (except the banana leaves) in a bowl and mix well. Rub the outside of the duck with some of the mixture and fill the cavity with the remainder. Close the opening with skewers.

Lay a large piece of foil on a flat surface and top with four large pieces of banana leaf. Place the duck in the centre, wrap to completely enclose and secure with kitchen string. Lay the duck on a rack in a large roasting tin and pour enough hot water into the tin to come halfway up the sides. Cover with foil, pressing around the edges to form a seal. Steam in the oven for 90 minutes, then open the foil and banana leaves to expose the duck. Return to the oven for a further 40 minutes, or until golden.

Unwrap the duck from the banana leaves and cut it into pieces — the meat should be so tender that it falls off the bones. Serve the duck meat and stuffing with steamed rice.

tip **The flavour of the duck is even better if the final cooking is done in a covered barbecue.**

stuffed golden nugget pumpkins

serves 4

4 large **golden nugget pumpkins**, about 600 g (1 lb 5 oz) each (see tip)
2 tablespoons **oil**
5 slices of **bacon**, chopped
1 **chorizo sausage**, roughly chopped
1 **red onion**, finely chopped
3 teaspoons **Moroccan seasoning**
150 g (5 1/2 oz/3 1/3 cups) **baby English spinach**
185 g (6 1/2 oz/1 cup) **couscous**
250 ml (9 fl oz/1 cup) boiling **water**
80 g (2 3/4 oz/1/2 cup) **pine nuts**, toasted
125 g (4 1/2 oz/1 cup) grated **cheddar cheese**
1 tablespoon snipped **chives**

Cut the top off each pumpkin and scoop out the seeds and membrane with a spoon.

Heat 1 tablespoon of oil in a frying pan over high heat and cook the bacon and chorizo for 4–5 minutes, or until brown. Stir in the onion and Moroccan seasoning and cook for a further 3 minutes, or until the onion has softened slightly. Toss in the spinach and cook for about 1 minute, or until wilted.

Put the couscous in a bowl, pour on the boiling water, then cover and set aside for 15 minutes. Fluff up the grains with a fork and stir in the bacon mixture, pine nuts and cheese. Season with salt and pepper and toss to combine. Fill each pumpkin with the couscous mixture, then replace the pumpkin tops.

Line a large steamer with baking paper and punch with holes. Place the pumpkins in a single layer on top and cover with a lid. Sit the steamer over a saucepan or wok of boiling water and steam for 35–40 minutes, or until the pumpkin is tender when pierced with a skewer. Serve with the tops to one side and garnish with chives.

tip **If you can't find the large golden nuggets, use eight small ones and reduce the cooking time to 30–35 minutes.**

sticky pork fillet

serves 4

3 tablespoons **Chinese rice wine**

3 tablespoons **char siu sauce**

2 tablespoons **hoisin sauce**

1 tablespoon **honey**

3 **garlic cloves**, finely chopped

1 tablespoon finely grated fresh **ginger**

1 teaspoon **Chinese five-spice**

1 teaspoon **sesame oil**

2 x 300 g (10 1/2 oz) **pork fillets**, halved

400 g (14 oz/1 bunch) **baby bok choy (pak choy)**, halved and rinsed

Combine the rice wine, sauces, honey, garlic, ginger, five-spice and sesame oil in a shallow dish. Add the pork and toss until well coated. Cover and leave to marinate overnight in the refrigerator.

Line the bottom basket of a double steamer with several pieces of baking paper and the top basket with a single layer. Punch the paper with holes. Lay the pork in a single layer in the bottom basket and cover with a lid. Sit the steamer over a wok or saucepan of boiling water and steam for about 20–25 minutes, basting the pork regularly.

Lay the bok choy in the top steamer basket, cover and steam both baskets for a further 5 minutes. Remove the pork and cover. Pour the remaining marinade into a small saucepan, stir in 1–2 tablespoons of water and simmer over high heat for 5 minutes to reduce slightly.

Slice the pork fillets and arrange on plates or in bowls with the bok choy. Drizzle with the sauce and serve immediately with steamed rice.

mahi mahi with roast tomatoes, feta and butterbeans

serves 4

6 **roma (plum) tomatoes**

150 g (5 1/2 oz) marinated **feta cheese**, plus 4 tablespoons of the oil marinade

2 tablespoons finely chopped **oregano**

1 teaspoon finely grated **lemon zest**

sea salt, to taste

4 x 200 g (7 oz) **mahi mahi** or any other **firm white fish fillets**, halved

250 g (9 oz) **baby green beans**, trimmed

400 g (14 oz) tin **butterbeans (lima beans)**, drained and rinsed

80 g (2 3/4 oz/1/2 cup) **ligurian olives**

1 handful **flat-leaf (Italian) parsley**

Preheat the oven to 200°C (400°F/Gas 6) and line a baking tray with baking paper. Place the tomatoes, cut side up, on the tray and drizzle with 1 tablespoon of the feta oil. Roast in the oven for 40 minutes. When the tomatoes are soft and starting to caramelize, remove from the oven and set aside.

Put the oregano, lemon zest, 2 tablespoons of the feta oil, sea salt and freshly ground black pepper in a small bowl and stir to combine. Cut out four 30 cm (12 inch) square sheets of baking paper. Place two pieces of fish side by side in the centre of each square and spoon on some of the oregano marinade. Carefully wrap the fillets into secure parcels so they don't leak, then place them in a large steamer in a single layer, seam side up, and cover with a lid.

Sit the steamer over a saucepan or wok of boiling water and steam for about 10–15 minutes, or until the fish flakes easily when tested with a fork. Using a spatula, carefully remove the parcels from the steamer and rest on a plate. Put the baby beans in the same steamer and cover with a lid. Steam for 7 minutes.

To serve, make a free-form stack with the fish fillets, roasted tomatoes, baby beans, butterbeans, olives, parsley and feta. Drizzle with any extra steamer juices plus the remaining feta oil and season with freshly ground black pepper.

vegetable, ricotta and prosciutto rolls

serves 4

8 **red** or **green cabbage leaves** (see tip)

iced **water**

30 g (1 oz) **butter**

1 **leek**, white part only, finely chopped

130 g (4 1/2 oz) **cauliflower**, chopped into 1.5 cm (5/8 inch) florets

2 **garlic cloves**, finely chopped

2 **anchovies**, drained and chopped

2 teaspoons finely chopped **oregano**

375 g (13 oz/1 1/2 cups) fresh **ricotta cheese**

50 g (1 3/4 oz) **goat's cheese**

35 g (1 1/4 oz/1/3 cup) finely grated **parmesan cheese**

1 **egg**

100 g (3 1/2 oz/2/3 cup) frozen **peas**

1 handful **basil**, chopped

1 teaspoon finely grated **lemon zest**

8 slices of **prosciutto**

Put the cabbage leaves in a saucepan of boiling water, then reduce the heat and simmer for 30–60 seconds, or until just tender and brightly coloured. Remove and plunge into iced water. Drain and pat dry. Remove the core if necessary.

Heat the butter in a non-stick frying pan over medium heat. Add the leek and cauliflower and cook, stirring, for 5 minutes. Add the garlic, anchovies and oregano and cook for a further 2 minutes, or until the anchovies have softened. Remove from the heat.

Combine the ricotta, goat's cheese, parmesan, egg, peas, basil and lemon zest in a bowl. Add the leek and cauliflower mixture and stir to combine. Season to taste.

To assemble, lay a slice of prosciutto in the centre of each cabbage leaf, with the longest sides at the top and bottom. Put 4 tablespoons of the cheese mixture on top of the proscuitto, about a third of the way up from the bottom. Roll the leaf once upwards, fold in the sides, then continue rolling until you have a 12 x 6 cm (4 1/2 x 2 1/2 inch) roll.

Line a steamer with baking paper and punch with holes. Arrange the rolls in a single layer on top and cover with a lid. Sit the steamer over a saucepan or wok of boiling water and steam for 25 minutes, or until cooked. Serve immediately with a rocket salad.

tip **To separate cabbage leaves easily, dip the whole cabbage into boiling water for 10–20 seconds.**

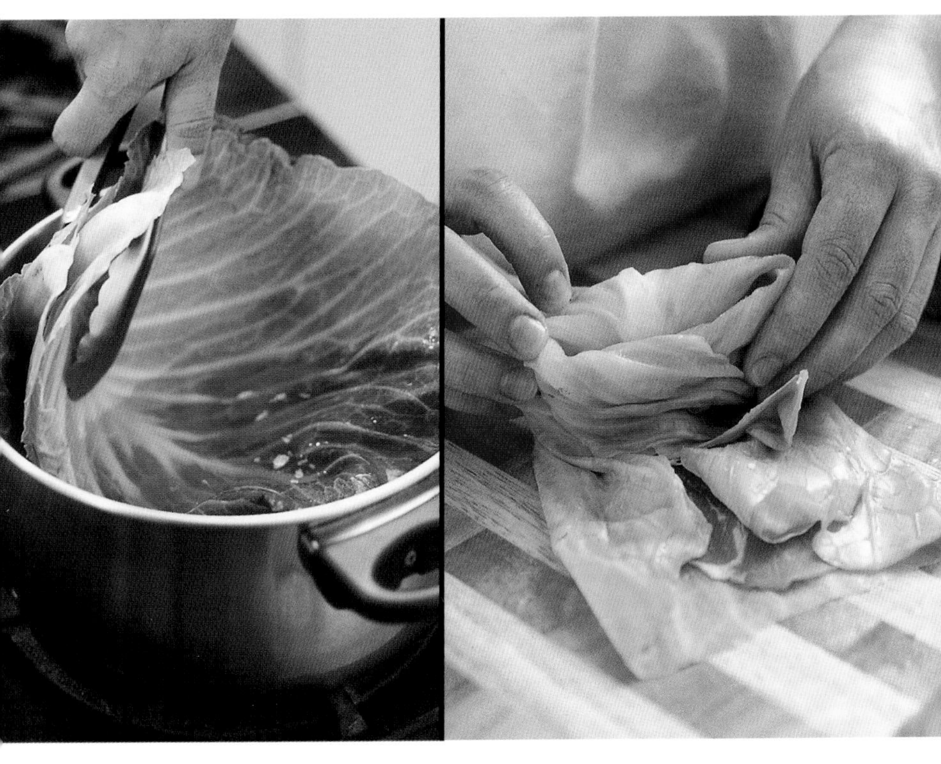

Simmer the **cabbage** leaves until just tender and **brightly coloured**.

Roll the cabbage leaf once, fold in the sides, then roll the rest of the leaf and **filling**.

barramundi with beetroot mash and dill and caper sauce

serves 4

30 **bay leaves**
2 **beetroot (beets)**, peeled and chopped into 4 cm (1 1/2 inch) pieces
3 **roasting potatoes**, chopped into 4 cm (1 1/2 inch) pieces
4 tablespoons **cream (whipping)**
2 teaspoons **aged balsamic vinegar**
100 g (3 1/2 oz) **butter**
1 **lemon**, sliced
4 **barramundi** or any **firm white fish fillets**
1 teaspoon **lemon juice**
3 teaspoons **baby salted capers**, rinsed and squeezed dry
3 teaspoons finely chopped **dill**

Line a large steamer with the bay leaves. Add the beetroot and cover with a lid. Sit the steamer over a saucepan or wok of boiling water and steam for 20 minutes. Add the potato and steam for a further 20 minutes, or until cooked through.

Put the beetroot and potato in a saucepan and quickly mash with the cream, vinegar and 20 g (3/4 oz) of the butter. Season well, and cover to keep warm.

Line a steamer with baking paper and punch with holes. Top with the lemon slices, then place the fish fillets on top in a single layer. Cover with a lid and steam for 5 minutes, or until cooked through when tested.

Meanwhile, melt the remaining butter in a non-stick frying pan over medium–low heat and cook for 3 minutes, or until the butter starts to brown. Add the lemon juice, capers and dill and stir until combined. Serve immediately drizzled over the fish and beetroot mash. Delicious with steamed greens.

lamb tagine with figs, eggplant and steamed couscous

serves 4

375 g (13 oz/2 cups) **couscous**
1 tablespoon **olive oil**
20 g (3/4 oz) **butter**
4 **lamb shanks**, french-trimmed (ask your butcher to do this for you)
1 **onion**, sliced
2 **garlic cloves**, finely chopped
1 teaspoon **ground ginger**
1 teaspoon **ground cumin**
1 teaspoon **sweet paprika**
1 **cinnamon stick**
500 ml (17 fl oz/2 cups) **chicken stock**
zest of 1/2 **lemon**, cut into 3 x 5 cm (1 1/4 x 2 inch) strips
1 large handful **coriander (cilantro) leaves**, chopped
165 g (5 3/4 oz/1 cup) **Turkish dried figs**, halved
2 long, thin **eggplants (aubergines)**,
chopped into 1.5 cm (5/8 inch) pieces
1 tablespoon **honey**
30 g (1 oz) **butter**, extra, chopped

Add the **chicken stock**, lemon zest, lamb shanks and half the coriander.

Cover the **couscous** with a clean tea towel and **steam** for 20 minutes.

Put the couscous in a large shallow bowl and cover with water. Stir, then pour off the water immediately into a strainer. Return the couscous to the bowl and set aside for 15 minutes to swell. Separate the grains with your fingers.

Heat the oil and butter in a large heavy-based saucepan over medium heat. Add the lamb shanks and cook for 3–4 minutes, or until lightly browned all over, then remove from the saucepan and set aside. Add the onion and cook for 3 minutes, or until softened. Stir in the garlic, ginger, cumin, paprika and cinnamon stick and cook for 30 seconds, or until fragrant. Add the chicken stock, lemon zest, lamb shanks and half the coriander and season well. Stir to combine, then cover and simmer over low heat for 1 hour, turning the lamb occasionally.

To steam the couscous over the lamb tagine, make sure the edges are sealed by placing a long strip of foil around the rim of the saucepan. Put the couscous in a strainer that is double-lined with muslin (cheesecloth). Sit the strainer on top of the saucepan and press down firmly. Cover with a tea towel (dish towel) and steam for 20 minutes.

Remove the strainer from the saucepan, add the figs, eggplant and honey and stir to combine. Replace the strainer, then add the extra butter, 1/4 teaspoon of salt and 4 tablespoons of water to the couscous. Fluff with a fork to combine and break up the grains, then cover and cook, stirring occasionally, for a further 20 minutes, or until cooked through. Skim off any excess fat. Spoon the couscous onto serving plates, top with the lamb tagine, and garnish with the remaining coriander.

gado gado kebabs on steamed rice

serves 4

200 g (7 oz/1 cup) **jasmine rice**
20 g (3/4 oz) **butter**
3 small **carrots**, chopped on the diagonal into 1 cm (1/2 inch) rounds
220 g (7 3/4 oz) **broccoli**, chopped into 4 cm (1 1/2 inch) florets
16 **makrut (kaffir lime) leaves**
5 **baby (pattypan) squash**, halved
150 g (5 1/2 oz) **cauliflower**, chopped into 4 cm (1 1/2 inch) florets
2 **zucchini (courgettes)**, each chopped on the diagonal into 4 pieces
1 1/2 tablepoons **Thai red curry paste**
250 ml (9 fl oz/1 cup) **coconut cream**
125 g (4 1/2 oz/1/2 cup) **crunchy peanut butter**
2 teaspoons grated **palm sugar** or **soft brown sugar**
1 tablespoon **lime juice**
2 teaspoons **fish sauce**
40 g (1 1/2 oz/1/2 cup) **bean sprouts**, trimmed
1 handful **coriander (cilantro) leaves**
1 handful **mint**
2 **spring onions (scallions)**, finely chopped on the diagonal
4 **eggs**, hard-boiled and halved

Wash the rice until the water runs clear, then put in a large saucepan with the butter, 1 teaspoon of salt and 435 ml (15 1/4 fl oz/1 3/4 cups) of water. Boil for 1 minute. Stir and cover tightly, then reduce the heat to very low and cook for 10 minutes. Turn off the heat and leave, covered, for 10 minutes. Fluff the rice with a fork.

For the kebabs, thread a piece of carrot followed by broccoli, lime leaf, squash, cauliflower, lime leaf, zucchini, carrot and broccoli onto a long wooden skewer. Repeat with the remaining vegetables to make eight skewers. Place the skewers in a large steamer and cover with a lid. Sit the steamer over a wok or saucepan of boiling water and steam for 7 minutes, or until just cooked through.

Cook the curry paste in a saucepan over low heat for 30 seconds, or until fragrant. Add the coconut cream, peanut butter, sugar, juice, fish sauce and 4 tablespoons of water and stir until heated through. Combine the bean sprouts, coriander, mint and spring onion in a bowl.

To serve, divide the rice among four bowls. Top with the sprout mixture, kebabs and peanut sauce. Garnish with the eggs and serve immediately.

slow-cooked lamb roast

serves 4–6

2 kg (4 lb 8 oz) **leg of lamb**, deboned (see tip)

2 tablespoons **olive oil**

1 teaspoon grated **lemon zest**

1 tablespoon **lemon juice**

2 tablespoons **dijon mustard**

2 tablespoons chopped **oregano**

4 **garlic cloves**, crushed

60 g (2 1/4 oz) **feta cheese**

750 ml (26 fl oz/3 cups) **chicken stock**

Preheat the oven to 160°C (315°F/Gas 2–3). Lay the leg of lamb out flat, skin side down. Combine the oil, lemon zest and juice, mustard, oregano and garlic and spread half of this mixture over the lamb. Crumble the feta over the top. Roll up the lamb tightly and secure with skewers and string.

Place the lamb, skin side down, on a rack and put the rack in a roasting tin. Pour the stock into the tin, then cover loosely with foil and steam for 1 hour 30 minutes.

Remove the foil, turn the lamb skin side up and spread with the remaining mustard mixture. Cook the lamb, uncovered, for 1 hour (for medium), or until cooked the way you like it.

Remove the lamb from the oven, re-cover with the foil, and rest for 15 minutes. Slice and drizzle with the pan juices. Serve with potato mash and steamed greens.

tip **Ask your butcher to debone the lamb for you.**

rolled chicken breasts with creamy leeks

serves 4

4 boneless, skinless **chicken breasts**

1 tablespoon **wholegrain mustard**

30 g (1 oz/2/3 cup) **baby English spinach**

80 g (23/4 oz) shaved **ham**

60 g (21/4 oz/1/2 cup) finely chopped **semi-dried (sun-blushed) tomatoes**

30 g (1 oz) **butter**

1 **leek**, white part only, sliced

2 **garlic cloves**, crushed

170 ml (51/2 fl oz/2/3 cup) **dry white wine**

125 ml (4 fl oz/1/2 cup) **thickened (whipping) cream**

Lay a chicken breast between two sheets of plastic wrap on a work surface. Flatten lightly with a meat tenderizer or rolling pin until it is about 1.5 cm (5/8 inch) thick. Repeat with the remaining chicken breasts. Spread the underside of the breasts with the mustard, top with the spinach and ham and sprinkle with the tomatoes. Roll each up tightly from the thick end, then wrap tightly in a sheet of plastic wrap, twisting the ends to seal well, then wrap again.

Place the rolls in a steamer and cover with a lid. Sit the steamer over a saucepan or wok of simmering water and cook for 15–20 minutes, or until the chicken feels just firm. Remove the rolls from the steamer and leave for 5 minutes before unwrapping and slicing thickly.

Meanwhile, melt the butter in a small saucepan over medium heat, add the leek and garlic and cook, stirring, for about 5 minutes, or until softened. Add the wine and simmer until reduced by half. Add the cream, bring to the boil and stir until the liquid has reduced by half. Spoon the creamy leeks with the chicken.

sweet potato and ricotta gow gees with rocket pesto

serves 4

250 g (9 oz) **orange sweet potato**, roughly chopped

1 **egg**, lightly beaten

125 g (4 1/2 oz/1/2 cup) fresh **ricotta cheese**

3 tablespoons grated **parmesan cheese**

1 tablespoon **lemon thyme**

3 tablespoons snipped **chives**

40 **round gow gee dumpling wrappers** (see tip)

rocket pesto

15 g (1/2 oz/2/3 cup) **rocket (arugula)**, roughly chopped

1 handful **basil**, roughly chopped

50 g (1 3/4 oz/1/3 cup) **pine nuts**

100 g (3 1/2 oz/heaped 1/3 cup) fresh **ricotta cheese**

2 tablespoons grated **parmesan cheese**

3 tablespoons **olive oil**

2 tablespoons **lemon juice**

Put the sweet potato in a steamer and cover with a lid. Sit the steamer over a saucepan or wok of boiling water and steam for about 15 minutes, or until tender. Transfer to a bowl and cool. Mash roughly with a fork, then stir in the egg, ricotta, parmesan, thyme and chives.

Take a gow gee wrapper and moisten the edge with water. Top with 1 level tablespoon of the sweet potato mixture and spread to within 1 cm (1/2 inch) of the edge. Top with another wrapper and press the edges together to seal. Place on a baking tray lined with baking paper and cover with a damp tea towel (dish towel). Repeat with the remaining wrappers and mixture. Refrigerate until ready to cook.

To make the pesto, combine all the ingredients in a food processor or mortar and pestle and blend until coarsely chopped.

Lay a quarter of the gow gees in a steamer in a single layer and cover with a lid. Sit the steamer over a saucepan or wok of simmering water and steam for 15 minutes, or until the wrappers have softened. Brush the wrappers liberally with water a couple of times during cooking. Remove, transfer to a baking tray and cover with foil to keep warm. Cook the remaining gow gees, then serve topped with the rocket pesto.

tip **Gow gee wrappers can be bought from the refrigerator section in most delicatessens and supermarkets. If the round wrappers are not available, use the square ones (also known as won ton wrappers). The gow gees can be prepared several hours ahead, but cook them just before serving.**

Put another **gow gee** wrapper over the filling and **press** the edges to seal.

Combine the rocket pesto ingredients and blend until **coarsely chopped**.

glazed spatchcocks

serves 4

4 **spatchcocks (poussin)**, rinsed and patted dry with paper towels

1 **lemon**, cut into wedges

8 **garlic cloves**, halved

3 tablespoons **plum sauce**

3 tablespoons **oyster sauce**

1 tablespoon **honey**

4 small **red chillies**, seeded and finely chopped

Preheat the oven to 200°C (400°F/Gas 6). Fill the cavity of each spatchcock with the lemon and garlic, then tie the legs together with string.

Place the spatchcocks on a rack, then put the rack in a roasting tin and pour in enough water to cover the base of the tin. Cover loosely with foil and bake for 30 minutes. Remove the foil.

Combine the plum sauce, oyster sauce, honey and chilli and brush over the spatchcocks. Return them to the oven and cook, uncovered, for 40 minutes, or until golden brown and the juices run clear when pierced with a knife. Brush occasionally with the marinade during cooking.

This is delicious served with steamed rice and green beans.

spicy veal balls in tomato sauce

serves 4

80 g (2 3/4 oz/1 cup) **fresh breadcrumbs**
3 tablespoons **milk**
500 g (1 lb 2 oz) **minced (ground) veal**
1 **garlic clove**, crushed
40 g (1 1/2 oz/1/4 cup) **pine nuts**, toasted and chopped
4 slices of **pancetta**, finely chopped
2 tablespoons finely chopped **oregano**
2 tablespoons finely chopped **flat-leaf (Italian) parsley**
2 **bird's eye chillies**, seeded and finely chopped
350 g (12 oz) **pappardelle**
25 g (1 oz/1/4 cup) shaved **parmesan cheese**

tomato sauce

2 tablespoons **olive oil**
1 **onion**, finely chopped
1 **garlic clove**, finely chopped
1/4 teaspoon **cayenne pepper**
800 g (1 lb 12 oz) tinned chopped **tomatoes**
1 teaspoon **caster (superfine) sugar**
1 tablespoon **tomato paste (concentrated purée)**
125 ml (4 fl oz/1/2 cup) **dry white wine**
2 large handfuls **baby English spinach**

Arrange the veal balls in a single layer in the **steamer**.

Pour in the **tomatoes**, sugar, tomato paste and wine and simmer over **low heat**.

Soak the breadcrumbs and milk in a large bowl for 10 minutes. Add the veal, garlic, pine nuts, pancetta, oregano, parsley, chilli, 1 teaspoon of salt and some freshly ground pepper. Use your hands to combine the ingredients then roll the mixture into balls the size of walnuts (this mixture is a little wet).

Line a large steamer with baking paper and punch with holes. Place the veal balls in the steamer in a single layer and cover with a lid. Sit the steamer over a saucepan or wok of boiling water and steam for 10 minutes, or until cooked.

To make the tomato sauce, heat the oil in a large frying pan over medium–high heat. Add the onion and cook, stirring occasionally, for 5 minutes, or until soft and lightly golden. Add the garlic, cayenne pepper and salt and pepper and cook for a further minute.

Pour in the tomatoes and add the sugar, tomato paste and white wine. Simmer the sauce over low heat for 15 minutes, stirring occasionally. Add the veal balls and cook, uncovered, for a further 10 minutes. Remove from the heat and stir in the spinach leaves.

Meanwhile, cook the pasta in a large saucepan of salted boiling water for about 8–10 minutes, or until *al dente*. Drain well, then divide the pasta among four bowls. Spoon the meatballs and sauce over the top and sprinkle with shaved parmesan.

herb and pistachio terrine

serves 8

200 g (7 oz) piece of **ham off the bone**, cut into 1 cm (1/2 inch) cubes

500 g (1 lb 2 oz) **minced (ground) veal**

500 g (1 lb 2 oz) **minced (ground) chicken**

165 g (53/4 oz/2 cups) **fresh white breadcrumbs**

2 tablespoons chopped **sage**

4 tablespoons snipped **chives**

50 g (13/4 oz/1/3 cup) unsalted **pistachio nuts**, roughly chopped

1 teaspoon **garam masala**

2 teaspoons grated **orange zest**

2 **garlic cloves**, crushed

2 tablespoons **tomato paste (concentrated purée)**

Preheat the oven to 180°C (350°F/Gas 4). Line a 23 x 13 cm (9 x 5 inch) loaf (bar) tin with baking paper.

Combine all the ingredients in a bowl, then press the mixture firmly into the loaf tin. Cover loosely with foil.

Place the loaf tin in a roasting tin, then pour enough hot water into the roasting tin to come halfway up the sides. Bake for 30 minutes, then remove the foil and cook for a further 30 minutes, or until the juices run clear. Remove from the oven and take out of the roasting tin.

If you are serving the terrine hot, turn it out, cut it into thick slices and serve with vegetables. If you prefer to eat it cold, allow it to cool in the tin before turning it out and serving with a salad.

potato gnocchi with spinach, orange and pine nuts

serves 4

gnocchi

500 g (1 lb 2 oz) **roasting (floury) potatoes**

85 g (3 oz/2/3 cup) **plain (all-purpose) flour**, sifted

2 tablespoons **olive oil**

30 g (1 oz) **butter**

finely grated zest and juice of 1 small **orange**

125 g (41/2 oz/5 cups) **baby English spinach**

3 tablespoons **pine nuts**, toasted

freshly shaved **parmesan cheese**, to serve

To make the gnocchi, cut the unpeeled potatoes into uniform pieces, roughly the size of a lemon. Arrange in a single layer in a large steamer and cover with a lid. Sit the steamer over a saucepan or wok of boiling water and steam for 25–30 minutes, or until the potatoes are tender but not breaking up. Transfer to a bowl and leave to cool. Cover loosely and refrigerate for 4 hours, or overnight. This helps to give a dry, light-textured dough.

Peel the potatoes and cut out any blemishes. Mash in a large bowl using a potato masher or ricer (don't do this in a blender or food processor as this will result in a starchy purée that won't form a light dough). Add a large pinch of salt and half the flour. With clean hands, lightly work it into the potatoes. When you have a mix dry enough to clump together, add the remaining flour and work it in to give a soft dough that is damp, but doesn't stick to your fingers. Transfer to a floured surface and lightly knead until it is smooth. Rest the dough for 5 minutes.

Pull off one-quarter of the dough and roll it with your hands to a long rope the thickness of your thumb. Cut this into 3 cm (1 1/4 inch) lengths. You can either leave the gnocchi as is, or roll each one in your hands into an egg shape. Repeat with the remaining dough.

Put the olive oil, butter, orange zest and orange juice in a large frying pan over medium heat until the butter melts. Remove from the heat and reserve.

Line a large steamer with baking paper and punch with holes. Spread half the gnocchi in a single layer on top and cover with a lid. Sit the steamer over a saucepan or wok of boiling water and steam for 5 minutes, or until the gnocchi are cooked. They will be slightly sticky on the outside at this stage so lightly flour your hands. Transfer to the frying pan and stir over medium heat to coat in the orange butter sauce. Repeat with the remaining gnocchi.

Add the spinach, increase the heat and cook, stirring, until the spinach wilts. Add the pine nuts and season with salt and freshly ground black pepper. Serve at once, with parmesan shavings.

tip **The gnocchi can be steamed in advance, spread on a tray to cool then heated in the orange butter when needed.**

Transfer the **dough** to a floured surface and lightly **knead** until it is smooth.

Roll the dough into a **long rope**, then cut it into short **lengths**.

duck, coconut and chilli rice parcels

serves 4

300 g (10 1/2 oz/1 1/2 cups) **basmati rice**
250 ml (9 fl oz/1 cup) **coconut cream**
8 pieces **banana leaf**, cut into 25 cm (10 inch) squares
boiling **water**, for blanching
1 **Chinese barbecued duck**
2 **long red chillies**, seeded and sliced
1 large handful **coriander (cilantro) leaves**
3 tablespoons **soy sauce**
2 teaspoons grated **palm sugar** or **soft brown sugar**
1 tablespoon finely grated fresh **ginger**
6 **spring onions (scallions)**, cut into 4 cm (1 1/2 inch) lengths

to serve

2 small **red chillies**, seeded and sliced
1 large handful **coriander (cilantro) leaves**
30 g (1 oz/1/2 cup) **fried shallots**
1 teaspoon **sesame oil**
lime wedges, to serve

Combine the rice, coconut cream and 375 ml (13 fl oz/1 1/2 cups) of water in a saucepan. Bring to the boil, then reduce the heat and simmer for 15–20 minutes, or until the rice is cooked and all the liquid is absorbed.

Blanch the banana leaves in boiling water for 1 minute to soften.

Remove the skin and flesh from the duck and shred finely. Place in a bowl with the chilli, coriander, soy sauce, palm sugar and ginger and toss to combine.

Spoon 70 g (2 1/2 oz/1/3 cup) of coconut rice onto a banana leaf, top with 50 g (1 3/4 oz/1/2 cup) of the duck mixture and lay two pieces of spring onion over this. Fold over the leaves to form a parcel and seal the ends with toothpicks. Repeat with the remaining ingredients to make eight parcels.

Line a steamer with baking paper and punch with holes. Arrange the parcels in a single layer on top and cover with a lid. Sit the steamer over a wok or saucepan of boiling water and steam for 15 minutes, or until heated through.

Open the banana leaves and garnish with the combined chilli, coriander, fried shallots and sesame oil. Serve two parcels per person with lime wedges.

stuffed turkey breast

serves 4

1 kg (2 lb 4 oz) double **turkey breast**, skin on

2 **garlic cloves**, crushed

4 slices of **prosciutto**

1 **mango**, peeled and diced

6 **sage leaves**

1 **rosemary** sprig, chopped

25 g (1 oz) unsalted **butter**, cut into cubes

2 tablespoons **olive oil**

375 ml (13 fl oz/1 1/2 cups) **chicken stock**

1 tablespoon **plain (all-purpose) flour**

Preheat the oven to 200°C (400°F/Gas 6). Put the turkey breast, skin side down, on a work surface. Push the underfillets (tenderloins) to one side, keeping them attached. Rub one crushed garlic clove all over the flesh of the breast. Cover the fillet with the prosciutto and place the mango, sage, rosemary, butter and some freshly ground pepper down the centre. Wrap the turkey around the stuffing so the skin remains on the outside. Seal the ends with poultry pins or skewers. Using kitchen string, tie the thick part of the breast tightly and continue to wrap the string around the breast fillet until it is evenly rolled.

Combine 1 tablespoon of olive oil and the remaining crushed garlic in a bowl. Rub this all over the rolled turkey breast and season with freshly ground black pepper.

Heat the remaining oil in a frying pan over high heat and sear the breast on all sides until browned. Put the breast in an oven bag, pour in 125 ml (4 fl oz/1/2 cup) of chicken stock and seal. Put the bag in a roasting tin and bake for 1 hour, or until the turkey breast is cooked through. Remove the turkey from the bag and rest in a warm place for 10–15 minutes.

Strain the liquid from the bag into a small saucepan over high heat. Add the flour and stir continuously for 2–3 minutes. Pour in the remaining stock, bring to the boil, then reduce the heat and simmer for 3 minutes, or until the sauce has thickened. Carve the breast and serve with the sauce and your favourite vegetables.

penne with spring vegetables and pesto

serves 4

basil pesto

225 g (8 oz/2 bunches) **basil**
80 g (2 3/4 oz/1/2 cup) **pine nuts**
1 **garlic clove**, roughly chopped
30 g (1 oz/1/3 cup) grated **pepper pecorino cheese**, plus extra, to serve (see tip)
1 **red chilli**, roughly chopped
185 ml (6 fl oz/3/4 cup) **olive oil**

200 g (7 oz) **broccoli** , chopped into florets
100 g (3 1/2 oz) **button mushrooms**, sliced
1 **carrot**, cut into julienne strips
175 g (6 oz/1 bunch) **asparagus**, trimmed and cut into 2 cm (3/4 inch) lengths
500 g (1 lb 2 oz) **penne**
1/2 **red capsicum (pepper)**, cut into julienne strips

To make the pesto, put the basil, pine nuts, garlic, pecorino and chilli in a food processor and blend until finely chopped. With the motor running, add the olive oil in a thin stream and process until well combined. Season to taste.

Line a large steamer with baking paper and punch with holes. Arrange the broccoli, mushrooms, carrot and asparagus in a single layer on top and cover with a lid. Sit the steamer over a saucepan or wok of simmering water and steam for about 4–5 minutes, or until just cooked.

Meanwhile, cook the penne in a large saucepan of rapidly boiling salted water for 8–10 minutes, or until *al dente*. Drain well and return to the pan. Add the steamed vegetables, capsicum and pesto to the pasta and mix well. Serve hot or cold with extra pecorino, if desired.

tip **Pepper pecorino cheese (also known as pecorino pepato) is available at good delicatessens or cheese shops. If you can't find it, regular pecorino works just as well.**

molluscs with wasabi butter

serves 4–6

1.5 kg (3 lb 5 oz) **pipis** and/or **clams (vongole)**
24 **black mussels** (see tip)
24 **oysters**, on the shell
lemon or **lime wedges**, to serve

wasabi butter

250 g (9 oz) **butter** at room temperature, cut into cubes
3–4 tablespoons **wasabi powder**
2 tablespoons **Japanese soy sauce**
1 tablespoon chopped **lime zest**
2 tablespoons **lime juice**
2 tablespoons finely snipped **chives**
1 tablespoon finely chopped **basil**
1 tablespoon finely chopped **coriander (cilantro) leaves**
1 tablespoon finely chopped **thyme**
1/4 teaspoon **smoked paprika**

Cover the pipis and clams with **cold water** to remove any unwanted sand.

Steam until the **oysters** are warmed through and the other **molluscs** have opened.

To purge the pipis and clams, place them in a large bowl and cover with cold water. Leave them for 2–4 hours, changing the water every hour. This will remove any unwanted sand.

Scrub the mussels with a stiff brush and pull out the hairy beards. Discard any broken mussels, or open ones that don't close when tapped on the bench. Rinse well before steaming.

To make the wasabi butter, beat the butter with electric beaters until almost white. Fold in the remaining ingredients until well combined, then cover and refrigerate until ready to use.

Put the oysters, mussels and strained pipis and clams in a double steamer in a single layer and cover with a lid. Sit the steamer over a wok or saucepan of boiling water and steam for 5–10 minutes, or until the oysters are warmed through and the other molluscs have opened. Discard any unopened molluscs.

Melt the wasabi butter in a small saucepan over medium heat. Arrange the cooked molluscs on a large serving plate and drizzle with the wasabi butter. Serve with lemon or lime wedges, a green salad and bread to soak up the buttery juices.

tip **If storing mussels, keep them in a cool place covered by a damp cloth, not in water, as they will drown. They will keep for about a day.**

pork and quince pot roast

serves 6

6-rib **pork loin**, skin removed

2 tablespoons **olive oil**

1 **onion**, finely diced

1 large **carrot**, cut into 2 cm (3/4 inch) cubes

2 **garlic cloves**, finely chopped

250 ml (9 fl oz/1 cup) **dry white wine**

2 **quinces**, peeled and quartered

1 tablespoon **oregano**

500 ml (17 fl oz/2 cups) **chicken stock**

1 tablespoon **dijon mustard**

60 g (21/4 oz) **butter**, softened

3 tablespoons **plain (all-purpose) flour**

Preheat the oven to 150°C (300°F/Gas 2). Trim the pork of excess fat and season with salt and pepper. Heat the oil in a stockpot or very large saucepan and brown the pork on all sides. Remove from the pan. Reduce the heat and cook the onion and carrot, stirring frequently, for 5 minutes, or until the onion is golden. Add the garlic and stir for 30 seconds, then add the wine, quince, oregano and stock. Return the pork to the pan, bring to the boil, then cover with a tight-fitting lid and cook in the oven for 1 hour 45 minutes, or until the pork is cooked and tender.

Remove the pork, wrap it in foil and leave to rest. Remove the quince and set aside. Skim any excess fat off the sauce and stir in the mustard.

Mix the butter and flour to a smooth paste and gradually add to the liquid in the pan. Stir over medium heat until it thickens.

Cut the pork between each bone and serve with the quince pieces and the sauce. Delicious with mashed potatoes.

chicken and seafood jambalaya

serves 6

3 tablespoons **olive oil**
300 g (10 1/2 oz) boneless, skinless **chicken thighs**, cut into 2 cm (3/4 inch) dice
1 **onion**, finely chopped
2 **garlic cloves**, finely chopped
1 **celery stalk**, finely diced
1 **red capsicum (pepper)**, finely diced
1 teaspoon **smoked paprika**
1/4 teaspoon **ground white pepper**
1/4 teaspoon **ground black pepper**
1/4 teaspoon **cayenne pepper**
1/2 teaspoon **dried thyme**
1/2 teaspoon **dried basil**
400 g (14 oz/2 cups) **long-grain rice**
1 litre (35 fl oz/4 cups) **chicken stock**
400 g (14 oz) tin chopped **tomatoes**
2 **bay leaves**
400 g (14 oz) small **raw prawns (shrimp)**, peeled and deveined
200 g (7 oz) **squid tubes**, cleaned, cut into 4 x 3 cm (1 1/2 x 1 1/4 inch) pieces and scored (see tip)
2 tablespoons **lemon juice**
3 tablespoons chopped **parsley**
2 **spring onions (scallions)**, green part only, finely sliced
Tabasco sauce, to serve
lemon wedges, to serve

Heat the oil in a large frying pan or paella pan over medium–high heat, add the chicken in batches and cook for 2–3 minutes, or until golden. Remove from the pan and set aside. Add the onion, garlic, celery, capsicum, spices and herbs and cook gently for 5 minutes, or until the vegetables are golden.

Add the rice to the pan and stir for 1–2 minutes, or until the rice is coated in the spices and appears glossy. Gently stir in the chicken stock, tomatoes and bay leaves, bring to the boil, then reduce the heat to low and cover with a lid or foil. Steam for 15–20 minutes, or until most of the liquid has been absorbed. Arrange the prawns, squid and chicken on top of the rice and replace the lid. Continue steaming over low heat for 10 minutes, or until all the liquid has been absorbed. Leave the jambalaya for 5 minutes, then stir it gently. Pour the lemon juice over the top and garnish with parsley and spring onion. Serve immediately with Tabasco sauce and lemon wedges.

tip **As your fishmonger to clean the squid for you.**

Add the onion, garlic, celery, capsicum, spices and herbs to the pan and cook until **golden**.

Arrange the prawns, **squid** and chicken on top of the **rice**.

lamb in the pot with juniper berries

serves 6

1 tablespoon **olive oil**

1 **onion**, finely chopped

2 **garlic cloves**, finely chopped

1 **carrot**, diced

1 **celery stalk**, diced

2 **bay leaves**

310 ml (10 3/4 fl oz/1 1/4 cups) **dry white wine**

125 ml (4 fl oz/1/2 cup) **chicken stock**

30–40 **juniper berries**

1 teaspoon chopped **rosemary**

1.5 kg (3 lb 5 oz) **leg of lamb**

1 tablespoon **balsamic vinegar**

Heat the oil in a large, heavy-based saucepan over medium heat, add the onion, garlic, carrot and celery and cook, stirring, for 5 minutes, or until lightly coloured.

Add the bay leaves, wine, stock, juniper berries, rosemary and lamb and bring to the boil. Reduce the heat to low, cover with a tight-fitting lid and simmer gently for 2 hours 30 minutes, or until the lamb is extremely tender and falling off the bone.

Remove the lamb and cover with foil to keep warm. Add the vinegar to the saucepan and simmer over medium heat until the sauce has reduced and thickened. Season and serve the lamb with the sauce.

stuffed squid with fish and spinach

serves 4

50 g (1 3/4 oz/1 cup) **baby English spinach**
250 g (9 oz) **redfish** or other **firm white fish fillets**, skin and bones removed
1 **egg**
3 tablespoons **thick (double/heavy) cream**
1 tablespoon **tomato paste (concentrated purée)**
1 tablespoon **lemon juice**
2 **garlic cloves**, roughly chopped
4 **raw prawns (shrimp)**, peeled, deveined and roughly chopped
8 small **squid tubes**, about 15 cm (6 inches) long
1 tablespoon finely chopped **basil**
lemon wedges, to serve

sauce

1 tablespoon **extra virgin olive oil**
2 **garlic cloves**, crushed
200 ml (7 fl oz) **dry white wine**
1 **bay leaf**
1/2 teaspoon **vegetable stock powder**
1 large **vine-ripened tomato**, peeled, seeded and finely diced
1 tablespoon **cream (whipping)**
a dash of **Tabasco sauce**, or to taste

Wash the spinach leaves, add to a saucepan over low heat and stir until wilted. Squeeze all excess moisture from the spinach and place in a food processor with the fish, egg, cream, tomato paste, lemon juice and garlic. Purée for 5 minutes, or until a smooth paste is formed. Stir in the prawns and season. Using a piping bag or a teaspoon, put the fish mixture inside the squid tubes and secure the open ends with toothpicks. Make sure the tubes are only two-thirds full as the squid will shrink as it cooks. Arrange the squid in a single layer on a plate that will fit inside a steamer, put the plate in the steamer and cover with a lid. Sit the steamer over a saucepan or wok of boiling water and steam for 25 minutes, or until cooked.

To make the sauce, heat the oil in a saucepan over medium heat. Cook the garlic for 1 minute, or until fragrant, then add the wine, bay leaf and stock powder. Bring to the boil, then reduce the heat and simmer for 5 minutes, or until reduced by a quarter. Add the tomato and simmer for 5 minutes, then stir in the cream and Tabasco sauce. Season to taste. Divide the sauce among serving plates, place the squid on top and sprinkle with basil. Serve with lemon wedges.

rocket and ricotta cannelloni

serves 4

1 tablespoon **olive oil**
3 **spring onions (scallions)**, finely chopped
100 g (3 1/2 oz/1 small bunch) **rocket (arugula)**, finely chopped
350 g (12 oz/1 1/3 cups) **ricotta cheese**
2 **egg yolks**
50 g (1 3/4 oz/1/2 cup) finely grated **parmesan cheese**
4 fresh **lasagne sheets**, halved

butter and sage sauce

60 g (2 1/4 oz) **unsalted butter**
10 g (1/4 oz/1/2 cup) **sage leaves**
2 **garlic cloves**, finely sliced
2 teaspoons **lemon juice**

Line the base of a large steamer with baking paper and punch with holes. Heat the oil in a frying pan over medium heat, add the spring onion and some salt and ground black pepper and cook gently for 5 minutes. Toss in the rocket and allow to wilt, then remove the frying pan from the heat and leave the mixture to cool a little.

Meanwhile, put the ricotta, egg yolks and parmesan in a bowl and stir well. Add the cooled onion and rocket mixture and stir again until well combined.

Cook the lasagne sheets in salted boiling water for 1 minute (you may need to do this in batches). Remove and lay separately on a board so they don't stick together.

Put 2 tablespoons of filling at the base of each lasagne square, then shape into a log. Gently roll up the sheet, making sure the filling doesn't spill out. Arrange the cannelloni in a single layer in the prepared steamer, brush with some water and cover with a lid. Sit the steamer over a saucepan or wok of boiling water and steam for 15 minutes, or until cooked through.

Meanwhile, to make the butter sauce, melt the butter in a small saucepan over medium heat. Add the sage leaves and cook for 2 minutes, or until the leaves are crisp and the butter is golden. Add the garlic and lemon juice and remove the pan from the heat immediately. Season to taste.

Divide the cannelloni among serving plates (two per person) and spoon on some of the butter sauce. Serve immediately.

seafood chowder

serves 6

400 g (14 oz) **smoked cod**
750 ml (26 fl oz/3 cups) **milk**
400 g (14 oz) **firm white fish fillets**
3 **boiling potatoes**, cut into 1 cm (1/2 inch) cubes
12 small **raw prawns (shrimp)**, peeled and deveined
3 tablespoons **olive oil**
3 **leeks**, white part only, finely chopped
2 **garlic cloves**, crushed
1 **celery stalk**, diced
1 **carrot**, diced
1 **zucchini (courgette)**, diced
125 ml (4 fl oz/1/2 cup) **dry white wine**
2 litres (70 fl oz/8 cups) **fish stock**
2 **bay leaves**
60 g (21/4 oz) **butter**
100 g (31/2 oz/heaped 3/4 cup) **plain (all-purpose) flour**
3 tablespoons chopped **parsley**

Place the cod on a plate with 125 ml (4 fl oz/1/2 cup) of the milk and cover with foil. Put the plate in a steamer and cover with a lid. Sit the steamer over a saucepan or wok of boiling water and steam for 10 minutes. Drain, reserving the milk.

Wrap the fish fillets in baking paper, place in the steamer and steam for 10 minutes. Break the cod and fish fillets into flakes. Steam the potatoes for 5 minutes, then add the prawns and steam for a further 3 minutes.

Heat 1 tablespoon of the oil in a saucepan over medium heat, add the leek, garlic, celery, carrot and zucchini and cook, stirring, for 3–4 minutes. Pour in the wine and cook for 5 minutes, or until the carrot has softened.

Put the stock and bay leaves in a large saucepan over high heat, bring to the boil, then reduce the heat and simmer for 10 minutes, or until the liquid has reduced by one-third, removing any scum that collects on the surface.

Heat the butter and remaining oil in a large saucepan over medium heat. Stir in the flour and cook for 1 minute. Remove from the heat and gradually whisk in the reserved steaming milk, reduced stock and remaining milk. Return to the heat and stir constantly until the mixture boils and thickens.

Add the flaked fish, prawns, potatoes and vegetable mixture and warm through. Season well, stir in the parsley and serve.

middle eastern duck breast

serves 4

4 **duck breasts**, skin on

3 tablespoons **olive oil**

1/2 **onion**, finely chopped

100 g (3 1/2 oz/1 cup) **walnuts**, roughly chopped

250 ml (9 fl oz/1 cup) **chicken stock**

1 1/4 tablespoons **pomegranate molasses** (see tip)

1 tablespoon **lemon juice**

2 1/2 teaspoons **soft brown sugar**

60 g (2 1/4 oz/2 cups) loosely packed **watercress**, trimmed

large handful **parsley**

1/2 **red onion**, finely sliced

2 tablespoons **honey**

1/2 teaspoon **ras el hanout** (see tip)

2 tablespoons chopped **coriander (cilantro) leaves**

dressing

1 1/2 tablespoons **lemon juice**

3 tablespoons **extra virgin olive oil**

1 **garlic clove**, crushed

Score the duck skin in a criss-cross pattern 1 cm (1/2 inch) apart, sprinkle with salt and place the breasts in a single layer on a plate. Put the plate in a steamer and cover with a lid. Sit the steamer over a saucepan or wok of simmering water and steam for 10–15 minutes, depending on the thickness of the duck and individual taste. The duck should remain pink in the centre. Remove and set aside.

Heat 2 tablespoons of the oil in a saucepan over medium heat, add the onion and cook, stirring, for 5 minutes, or until soft. Add the walnuts, stir to coat in the oil for 2 minutes, then pour in the stock. Bring to the boil, then reduce the heat to low and simmer for 15–20 minutes. Add the pomegranate molasses, lemon juice and sugar and purée using a stick blender or regular blender. Continue to cook the sauce, stirring, for 1–2 minutes, or until thickened to a mayonnaise consistency.

Mix together the dressing ingredients and place in a bowl with the watercress, parsley and red onion. Toss gently until well coated.

In a small saucepan gently heat the honey and ras el hanout. Heat the remaining oil in a frying pan over medium heat, place the duck, skin side down, in the pan and cook for 3–4 minutes, or until the fat starts to render and the skin becomes golden. Remove the breasts from the pan and drain off the oil. Brush both sides with the honey mixture, then return to the pan and cook for 1 minute each side.

Allow the duck to rest for a few minutes before slicing. Spoon some walnut sauce on each plate and sprinkle with coriander, place the sliced duck on top and serve with the watercress salad.

tips **Pomegranate molasses is a richly concentrated syrup and is available in the Middle Eastern section of speciality food stores and in some larger supermarkets. Ras el hanout is a North African blend of spices. If you can't find it, use garam masala instead.**

Using a sharp **knife**, score the duck skin in a **criss-cross** pattern.

Cook the **duck** until the fat starts to render and the skin becomes **golden**.

steamed swordfish with risoni and herb pesto

serves 6

400 g (14 oz/2 cups) **risoni**

2 tablespoons **olive oil**

2 teaspoons grated **lemon zest**

6 x 175 g (6 oz) **swordfish steaks**, halved horizontally

90 g ($3\frac{1}{4}$ oz/2 cups) **baby English spinach**

1 **lemon**, cut into wedges

herb pesto

1 large handful **basil**

1 large handful **parsley**

50 g ($1\frac{3}{4}$ oz/1 heaped cup) **baby English spinach**

50 g ($1\frac{3}{4}$ oz/$\frac{1}{3}$ cup) **pistachio nuts**

40 g ($1\frac{1}{2}$ oz) **parmesan cheese**, chopped

2 **garlic cloves**, chopped

1 tablespoon finely grated **lemon zest**

4 tablespoons **olive oil**

Put the risoni, 1 tablespoon of olive oil and 1.125 litres (39 fl oz/$4\frac{1}{2}$ cups) of water in a saucepan and cover with a lid. Bring to the boil over high heat, then reduce the heat to very low and simmer for 12 minutes, or until the pasta is just *al dente* and there is barely any liquid in the pan. Spoon into a large bowl and keep warm.

Combine the lemon zest, remaining oil and salt and pepper in a non-metallic bowl, add the swordish and gently toss in the mixture. Cover and leave to marinate.

Meanwhile, to make the pesto, put all the ingredients except for the oil in a food processor. Pulse until roughly chopped (not too smooth), then tip into a bowl and stir in the olive oil. Season with salt and freshly ground pepper. Stir the pesto through the cooked pasta, then fold in the baby spinach — it will start to wilt in the heat of the pasta. Season to taste and keep warm.

Line a steamer with baking paper and punch with holes. Add the swordfish steaks and cover with a lid. Steam for 8–10 minutes, then remove and rest for 2 minutes.

Divide the pasta among serving plates and top each with two pieces of swordfish. Sprinkle with extra pepper and serve with a wedge of lemon.

carrot and parsnip roulade

serves 6

2 small **carrots**, roughly chopped
1 **parsnip**, roughly chopped
20 g (3/4 oz) **butter**
10 **sage leaves**, roughly chopped
1 tablespoon roughly chopped **flat-leaf (Italian) parsley**
4 **eggs**, separated
50 g (1 3/4 oz/1/2 cup) finely grated **parmesan cheese**
250 g (9 oz/1 cup) **ricotta cheese**
2 tablespoons snipped **chives**

Lightly grease a 33 x 25 cm (13 x 10 inch) Swiss roll tin (jelly roll tin) and line the base and sides with baking paper. Preheat the oven to 190°C (375°F/Gas 5).

Put the carrot and parsnip in a single layer in a steamer and cover with a lid. Sit the steamer over a saucepan or wok of boiling water and steam for 20 minutes, or until the vegetables have softened. Transfer to a food processor, add the butter, sage and parsley and process until smooth. Season, add the egg yolks and process to combine. Tip the mixture into a large bowl.

In a separate clean bowl beat the egg whites until soft peaks form. Using a large metal spoon fold a quarter of the egg white into the carrot mixture, then add the rest, stirring gently until just combined. Spoon into the prepared tin and smooth the surface. Bake for 15 minutes, or until it starts to turn golden.

Turn the roulade onto a greased sheet of baking paper placed over a tea towel (dish towel), then remove the bottom sheet of baking paper. Sprinkle with half the parmesan and allow to cool slightly.

Mix together the ricotta, chives and remaining parmesan and season to taste. Spread the mixture evenly over the roulade and roll it lengthways like a Swiss roll (jelly roll), using the baking paper to gently roll it. Serve immediately with steamed greens or a tossed salad.

fish cutlets with ginger and chilli

serves 4

4 x 175 g (6 oz) **firm white fish cutlets**, such as snapper or blue-eye
5 cm (2 inch) piece of **ginger**, shredded
2 **garlic cloves**, chopped
4 **red chillies**, seeded and chopped
2 tablespoons chopped **coriander (cilantro) stems**
3 **spring onions (scallions)**, cut into short, fine shreds
2 tablespoons **lime juice**

Line a steamer with banana leaves or baking paper and punch with holes. Place the fish in the steamer, top with the ginger, garlic, chilli and coriander and cover with a lid. Sit the steamer over a wok or saucepan of boiling water and steam for about 8–10 minutes, or until the fish flakes easily.

Sprinkle the spring onion and lime juice over the fish, cover and steam for an extra 30 seconds. Serve with steamed jasmine rice.

chicken breast with asian greens and soy mushroom sauce

serves 4

2 large dried **shiitake mushrooms**
4 tablespoons boiling **water**
2 tablespoons **light soy sauce**
2 tablespoons **Chinese rice wine**
1/2 teaspoon **sesame oil**
1 tablespoon finely sliced fresh **ginger**
4 x 200 g (7 oz) boneless, skinless **chicken breasts**
450 g (1 lb) **bok choy (pak choy)**, ends removed and cut lengthways into quarters
250 ml (9 fl oz/1 cup) **chicken stock**
1 tablespoon **cornflour (cornstarch)**

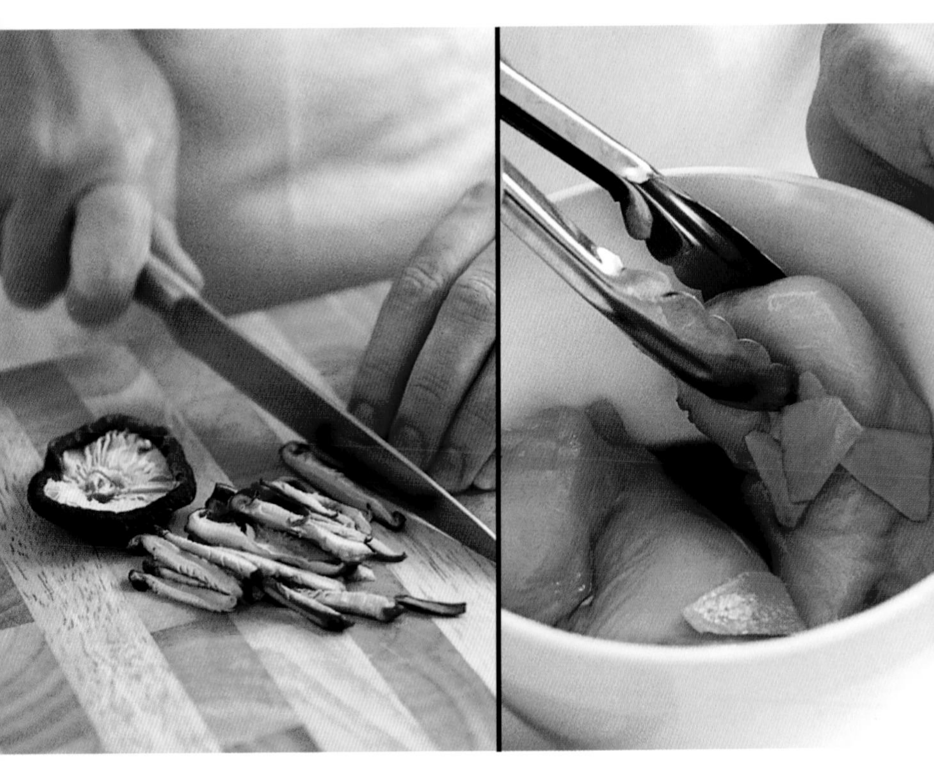

Remove the stalks from the **shiitake** mushrooms and finely slice the caps.

Add the **chicken** to the marinade, cover and **chill** for 1 hour.

Soak the dried mushrooms in the boiling water for 20 minutes. Drain, reserving the soaking liquid. Discard the stalks and finely slice the caps.

Combine the soy sauce, rice wine, sesame oil and ginger in a non-metallic dish. Add the chicken and turn to coat. Cover and marinate in the refrigerator for 1 hour.

Line a steamer with baking paper and punch with holes. Place the chicken on top, reserving the marinade, and cover with a lid. Sit the steamer over a wok or saucepan of boiling water and steam for 6 minutes, then turn the chicken over and steam for a further 6 minutes. Place the bok choy on top of the chicken and steam for 2–3 minutes.

Meanwhile, put the reserved marinade, mushrooms and the soaking liquid in a small saucepan and bring to the boil. Add enough stock to the cornflour in a small bowl to make a smooth paste. Add the cornflour paste and remaining stock to the pan and stir over medium heat for 2 minutes, or until the sauce thickens.

Arrange the chicken fillets and bok choy on serving plates, pour the sauce over the top and serve with steamed rice.

whole snapper with asian flavours

serves 2

800 g (1 lb 12 oz) whole **snapper**, scaled and gutted

3 **lemon grass stems**

1 handful **coriander (cilantro) leaves**

3 cm (1 1/4 inch) piece of **ginger**, cut into thin matchsticks

1 large **garlic clove**, cut into thin slivers

2 tablespoons **soy sauce**

3 tablespoons **oil**

1 tablespoon **fish sauce**

1 small **red chilli**, seeded and finely chopped

Score the fish with diagonal cuts on both sides. Cut each stem of lemon grass into three and lightly squash each piece with the end of the handle of a large knife. Put half the lemon grass in the middle of a large piece of foil and lay the fish on top. Put the remaining lemon grass and half the coriander leaves in the cavity of the fish.

Mix the ginger, garlic, soy sauce, oil, fish sauce and chilli together, then drizzle the mixture over the fish.

Enclose the fish in the foil, place it in a large steamer and cover with a lid. Sit the steamer over a wok or saucepan of boiling water and steam for 25 minutes, or until the flesh of the fish is opaque and white. Scatter with the remaining coriander leaves and serve with stir-fried Asian greens and steamed rice.

tofu with soy

serves 4

2 tablespoons **soy sauce**

2 tablespoons **kecap manis** (see tip)

1 teaspoon **sesame oil**

500 g (1 lb 2 oz) firm **tofu**, drained

1 1/2 teaspoons fresh **ginger**, cut into thin matchsticks

3 **spring onions (scallions)**, finely sliced on the diagonal

1 large handful **coriander (cilantro) leaves**, chopped

1–2 tablespoons **fried shallots**

Combine the soy sauce, kecap manis and sesame oil in a bowl. Cut the tofu in half widthways, then into triangles. Place on a heatproof plate and pour the sauce over the top. Marinate for 30 minutes, turning the tofu once.

Sprinkle the ginger over the tofu. Place the plate on a wire rack over a wok of boiling water and cover with a lid. Steam for 3–4 minutes, then sprinkle with the spring onion and coriander and steam for 3 minutes more. Garnish with the fried shallots and serve immediately.

tip **Kecap manis is a thick, sweet Indonesian soy sauce. It is readily available in Asian food stores and in the Asian section of larger supermarkets.**

jasmine tea steamed fish

serves 4

200 g (7 oz/2 2/3 cups) **jasmine tea leaves**
100 g (3 1/2 oz) **ginger**, finely sliced
4 **spring onions (scallions)**, cut into 5 cm (2 inch) lengths
4 x 200 g (7 oz) **firm white fish fillets** (such as snapper, barramundi or blue-eye)

ginger and spring onion sauce

125 ml (4 fl oz/1/2 cup) **fish stock**
3 tablespoons **light soy sauce**
3 **spring onions (scallions)**, finely sliced
1 tablespoon finely shredded fresh **ginger**
2 teaspoons **sugar**
1 large **red chilli**, seeded and sliced

Line a double steamer with baking paper and punch with holes. Arrange the tea, ginger and spring onion in the bottom basket and cover with a lid. Sit the steamer over a wok or saucepan of boiling water and steam for 10 minutes, or until the tea is moist and fragrant.

Lay the fish fillets in a single layer in the top basket and cover with the lid. Steam for 5–10 minutes, depending on the thickness of the fillet. To test for doneness, insert a skewer into the thickest part of the fillet — there should be no resistance. Remove from the steamer.

Meanwhile, to make the sauce, combine all the ingredients and 125 ml (4 fl oz/ 1/2 cup) of water in a small saucepan and stir over low heat for 5 minutes, or until the sugar has dissolved. Drizzle the sauce over the fish and serve with steamed rice and your favourite Asian greens.

japanese-style salmon parcels

serves 4

4 x 150 g (5 1/2 oz) **salmon steaks** or **cutlets**

2.5 cm (1 inch) piece **ginger**

2 **celery stalks**

4 **spring onions (scallions)**

1/4 teaspoon **dashi granules** (see tip)

3 tablespoons **mirin** (see tip)

2 tablespoons **tamari** (see tip)

2 teaspoons **sesame seeds**, toasted

Preheat the oven to 230°C (450°F/Gas 8). Cut four squares of baking paper large enough to enclose the salmon steaks.

Wipe the salmon and pat dry with paper towels. Place a salmon steak in the centre of each paper square.

Cut the ginger into paper-thin slices. Slice the celery and spring onions into short lengths, then lengthways into fine strips. Arrange a bundle of celery and spring onion and several slices of ginger on each salmon steak.

Combine the dashi, mirin and tamari in a small saucepan and heat gently until the granules dissolve. Drizzle over each salmon parcel, sprinkle with sesame seeds and carefully wrap the salmon, folding in the sides to seal in all the juices. Arrange the parcels on a baking tray and cook for about 12 minutes, or until tender. (The paper will puff up when the fish is cooked.) Do not overcook or the salmon will dry out. Serve immediately, as standing time can spoil the fish.

tip **Dashi, mirin and tamari are all available from Japanese food stores and most large supermarkets.**

crab with spices, coriander and chilli

serves 4

4 small or 2 large **live crabs**

2 **garlic cloves**, very finely chopped

2 teaspoons finely grated fresh **ginger**

1/4 teaspoon **ground cumin**

1/4 teaspoon **ground coriander**

1/4 teaspoon **ground turmeric**

1/4 teaspoon **cayenne pepper**

1 tablespoon **tamarind purée**

1 teaspoon **sugar**

2 small **red chillies**, seeded and finely chopped

125 ml (4 fl oz/1/2 cup) **oil**

2 tablespoons chopped **coriander (cilantro) leaves**

Put the crabs in the freezer for 1 hour to immobilize them. Using a large heavy-bladed knife or cleaver, cut the crabs in half (or quarters if you are using the large ones) and scrape out the spongey grey gills, then twist off and crack the claws. Turn the body over and pull off the apron pieces. Rinse well under cold running water and pat dry.

Arrange the crabs in a single layer in a large steamer and cover with a lid. Sit the steamer over a wok or saucepan of boiling water and steam for 4–5 minutes, or until half cooked. Remove from the heat.

Mix together the garlic, ginger, cumin, ground coriander, turmeric, cayenne pepper, tamarind, sugar, chilli, half the oil and a generous pinch of salt. Heat the remaining oil in a large deep frying pan over medium heat. When the oil is hot, add the spice mixture and stir for 30 seconds.

Add the crabs and cook, stirring, for 2 minutes, making sure the spice mix gets rubbed into the cut edges of the crab. Add 125 ml (4 fl oz/1/2 cup) of water, then cover and steam the crabs for a further 5–6 minutes, or until cooked. The crabs will turn pink or red when they are ready and the flesh will turn opaque. Drizzle a little of the liquid from the pan over the crabs and scatter with the coriander leaves. Serve with crab crackers, picks, finger bowls and bread.

tip **This recipe also works well with large prawns (shrimp).**

chicken tamales

serves 4

dough

100 g (3 1/2 oz) **butter**, softened

1 **garlic clove**, crushed

1 teaspoon **ground cumin**

210 g (7 1/2 oz/1 1/2 cups) **masa harina** (see tip)

4 tablespoons **cream (whipping)**

4 tablespoons **chicken stock**

filling

1 **corn cob**

2 tablespoons **oil**

150 g (5 1/2 oz) boneless, skinless **chicken breast**

2 **garlic cloves**, crushed

1 **red chilli**, seeded and chopped

1 **red onion**, chopped

1 **red capsicum (pepper)**, chopped

2 **tomatoes**, peeled and chopped

sour cream, to serve

chopped **coriander (cilantro) leaves**, to serve

To make the dough, beat the butter with electric beaters until creamy. Add the garlic, cumin and 1 teaspoon of salt and mix well. Add the masa harina and combined cream and stock alternately, beating until combined.

To make the filling, cook the corn in a saucepan of boiling water for 5–8 minutes, or until tender. Cool, then cut off the kernels with a sharp knife. Heat the oil in a frying pan and cook the chicken for about 5 minutes each side, or until golden. Remove, cool and shred finely. Add the garlic, chilli and onion to the pan and cook for 2–3 minutes, or until soft. Stir in the capsicum and corn and cook for 3 minutes. Add the chicken, tomato and 1 teaspoon of salt and simmer for 15 minutes, or until the liquid has reduced.

Cut 12 pieces of baking paper into 20 x 15 cm (8 x 6 inch) pieces. Spread a thick layer of dough over each piece, leaving a border at each end. Spoon some filling in the centre, roll up and secure with string. Arrange the parcels in a large steamer in a single layer and cover with a lid. Sit the steamer over a large saucepan or wok of boiling water and steam for 35 minutes, or until firm.

Arrange three tamales on each plate and serve with sour cream and coriander, and a fresh salad.

tip **Masa harina is a type of cornflour (cornstarch) and is readily available in larger supermarkets and health-food stores.**

Add the **chicken**, tomato and salt and simmer until the **liquid** has reduced.

Roll up the filled **parcels** and **secure** with string.

lemon grass chicken and rice rolls

serves 4

4 **lemon grass stems**, halved lengthways

3 boneless, skinless **chicken breasts**, halved lengthways

1 tablespoon **sesame oil**

2 **red chillies**, seeded and chopped

300 g (10 1/2 oz) **Chinese broccoli**, halved

300 g (10 1/2 oz) plain **rice noodle rolls** (see tip)

soy sauce, to serve

lime wedges, to serve

Arrange the lemon grass in a steamer. Place the chicken on top, brush with the sesame oil and sprinkle with chilli. Cover with a lid. Sit the steamer over a wok or saucepan of boiling water and steam for 5 minutes, or until half cooked.

Place the Chinese broccoli and rice noodle rolls in another steamer of the same size and sit it on top of the steamer with the chicken. Cover with a lid and steam for a further 5 minutes, or until the chicken is cooked and the broccoli is tender. Cut the chicken into thick slices and serve with the broccoli, noodle rolls, small bowls of soy sauce and wedges of lime.

tip **Rice noodle rolls are fresh blocks of thin rice noodles that have been rolled into a sausage shape. They are available at Asian food stores.**

beef pot roast

serves 6

300 g (10 1/2 oz) **baby onions**

boiling **water**, for soaking

30 g (1 oz) **butter**

2 **carrots**, cut into even-sized pieces

3 **parsnips**, cut into even-sized pieces

1.3 kg (3 lb) piece **eye of silverside**, trimmed of fat (see tip)

3 tablespoons **dry red wine**

1 large **tomato**, finely chopped

250 ml (9 fl oz/1 cup) **beef stock**

mustard, to serve

Put the onions in a heatproof bowl and cover with boiling water. Leave for 1 minute, then drain well. Allow to cool and then peel off the skins.

Heat half the butter in a large heavy-based saucepan that will tightly fit the meat (it will shrink during cooking), add the onions, carrot and parsnip and cook, stirring, over medium–high heat until browned. Remove from the pan.

Heat the remaining butter in the pan over medium heat, add the meat and brown well all over. Increase the heat to high and pour in the wine. Bring to the boil, then return the vegetables to the pan. Stir in the tomato and stock, return to the boil, then reduce the heat to low and simmer, covered, for 1 hour, turning once.

Remove the meat from the pan and put it on a board ready for carving. Cover with foil and leave it to stand while you finish the sauce.

Increase the heat to high and boil the pan juices with the vegetables for 10 minutes to reduce and thicken slightly. Skim off any fat and check the seasoning. Serve the meat and vegetables with the pan juices and some mustard.

tip **Eye of silverside is a tender, long-shaped cut of silverside that carves easily into serving-sized pieces. A regular piece of silverside or topside may be substituted.**

thai ginger fish with coriander butter

serves 4

60 g (2 1/4 oz) **butter**, at room temperature

1 tablespoon finely chopped **coriander (cilantro) leaves**

2 tablespoons **lime juice**

1 tablespoon **vegetable oil**

1 tablespoon grated **palm sugar** or **soft brown sugar**

4 **long red chillies**, seeded and chopped

2 **lemon grass stems**, trimmed and halved

4 x 200 g (7 oz) **firm white fish fillets** (such as blue-eye or john dory)

1 **lime**, finely sliced

1 tablespoon finely shredded fresh **ginger**

Thoroughly mix the butter and coriander together and roll it into a log. Wrap the log in plastic wrap and chill in the refrigerator for at least 30 minutes, or until you are ready to serve.

Combine the lime juice, oil, sugar and chilli in a small non-metallic bowl and stir until the sugar has dissolved.

Lay a piece of lemon grass in the centre of a sheet of foil large enough to fully enclose one fish fillet. Place a fish fillet on top and smear the surface with the lime juice mixture. Top with some lime slices and ginger shreds, then wrap into a secure parcel. Repeat with the remaining ingredients to make four parcels.

Line a large steamer with baking paper and punch with holes. Lay the fish parcels on top in a single layer and cover with a lid. Sit the steamer over a wok or saucepan of boiling water and steam for 8–10 minutes, or until the fish flakes easily when tested with a fork.

To serve, place the parcels on individual serving plates and serve open with slices of coriander butter and some steamed rice and green vegetables.

thai mussels with noodles

serves 4

2 kg (4 lb 8 oz) **mussels**

235 g (8 1/2 oz/4 small bundles) **glass noodles**

boiling **water**, for soaking

2 **garlic cloves**, crushed

2 **spring onions (scallions)**, finely chopped

125 ml (4 fl oz/1/2 cup) **fish stock**

2 tablespoons **Thai red curry paste**

170 ml (5 1/2 fl oz/2/3 cup) **coconut cream**

juice of 2 **limes**

2 tablespoons **fish sauce**

1 handful **coriander (cilantro) leaves**

Rinse the mussels in cold water and pull out the hairy beards. Discard any broken mussels, or open ones that don't close when tapped on a bench. Soak the noodles in boiling water for 8–10 minutes. Drain and, using a pair of scissors, cut them into shorter lengths.

Put the mussels, garlic and spring onion in a large steamer and cover with a lid. Sit the steamer over a wok or saucepan of boiling water and steam for 4–5 minutes, or until they are all open. Throw away any mussels that don't open.

Pour the fish stock into a large saucepan, add the curry paste and coconut cream and stir together. Bring the mixture to the boil, then add the lime juice and fish sauce. Put the mussels back in the pan, cook for 1 minute, then stir in the coriander.

Divide the noodles among bowls and ladle the mussels and broth over the top.

sides

broccoli and broad bean rice pilaff

serves 4–6

250 g (9 oz/1 1/4 cups) **basmati rice**

560 ml (19 1/4 fl oz/2 1/4 cups) **chicken stock**

350 g (12 oz) **broccoli**, chopped into bite-sized florets

310 g (11 oz/2 cups) frozen **broad (fava) beans**, shelled

6 **spring onions (scallions)**, finely chopped

1 teaspoon **sweet paprika**

2 handfuls **parsley**, roughly chopped

50 g (1 3/4 oz/1/3 cup) toasted **almonds**, roughly chopped

1 **garlic clove**, crushed

2 tablespoons **almond oil** or **extra virgin olive oil**

2 teaspoons finely grated **lemon zest**

3 tablespoons **medium-dry sherry**

Place the rice in a saucepan over medium–high heat, pour in the stock and cover with a lid. Bring to the boil, then reduce the heat to very low and simmer for about 8–10 minutes, or until the rice has absorbed all the liquid and is perfectly steamed.

Meanwhile, put the broccoli and broad beans in a steamer and cover with a lid. Sit the steamer over a saucepan or wok of boiling water and steam for 3 minutes. When the vegetables are still slightly undercooked, remove from the heat. Refresh the broad beans under cold water and peel.

Spoon the hot rice into a large bowl, add the vegetables, spring onion, paprika, parsley, almonds, garlic, almond oil, lemon zest and sherry. Season with salt and pepper and toss with a large spoon until well combined. This is delicious served with grilled fish and poultry or simply on its own.

wild rice with pumpkin

serves 4–6

190 g (6 3/4 oz/1 cup) **wild rice**, rinsed

300 g (10 1/2 oz) **jap (kent) pumpkin**, skin on, cut into 1 x 6 cm (1/2 x 2 1/2 inch) wedges

400 g (14 oz) tin **chickpeas**, drained and rinsed

8 **spring onions (scallions)**, finely sliced

50 g (1 3/4 oz/1/3 cup) **currants**

70 g (2 1/2 oz/1/2 cup) **pistachio nuts**, roughly chopped

1 teaspoon **garam masala**

3 tablespoons **pepitas (pumpkin seeds)**

2 tablespoons **pistachio oil** or **olive oil**

2 teaspoons finely grated **orange zest**

1 large handful **coriander (cilantro) leaves**

1 large handful **mint**, torn

Put the rice in a small saucepan over medium–high heat, add 625 ml (21 1/2 fl oz/ 2 1/2 cups) of water and cover with a lid. Bring to the boil, then reduce the heat to low and simmer for 30–35 minutes, or until all of the liquid has been absorbed and the rice is cooked but still *al dente*.

Line a steamer with baking paper and punch with holes. Arrange the pumpkin on top and cover with a lid. Sit the steamer over a saucepan or wok of boiling water and steam for 5 minutes, or until the pumpkin is tender when pierced with a sharp knife. Set aside to cool a little.

Put the chickpeas, spring onion, currants, pistachios, garam masala, pepitas, oil, orange zest, coriander and mint leaves in a large bowl and season with salt and pepper. Add the steamed rice and pumpkin wedges and toss gently to combine. Arrange the salad in a bowl or on a platter and serve warm.

caramelized onions and lentils with english spinach

serves 6

225 g (8 oz/1 1/4 cups) **puy lentils** or tiny **blue-green lentils**

3 tablespoons **olive oil**

2 **red onions**, finely sliced

2 **garlic cloves**, finely chopped

1 teaspoon **ground coriander**

1 teaspoon **ground cumin**

550 g (1 lb 4 oz) **English spinach**, rinsed well and stems trimmed

1 tablespoon **lemon juice**

2 tablespoons chopped **coriander (cilantro) leaves**

Put the lentils in a small saucepan over high heat, add 625 ml (21 1/2 fl oz/2 1/2 cups) of water and cover with a fitted lid. Bring to the boil, then reduce the heat to very low and simmer the lentils for 35 minutes, or until all of the water has been absorbed and the lentils are tender.

Meanwhile, heat the oil in a frying pan over medium heat and cook the onion, stirring occasionally, for 20 minutes, or until soft and caramelized. Add the garlic, ground coriander and cumin, season with salt and freshly ground black pepper and cook for a further 3 minutes. Remove from the heat.

Put the spinach in a large steamer and cover with a lid. Sit the steamer over a saucepan or wok of boiling water and steam for 3–5 minutes, or until wilted.

Combine the lentils, onion mixture and spinach in a large bowl, add the lemon juice and coriander and toss well. Serve immediately.

herb and spice couscous

serves 6

370 g (13 oz/2 cups) **couscous**

60 g (2 1/4 oz) **butter**

2 **spring onions (scallions)**, chopped

1 **garlic clove**, crushed

2 teaspoons **cumin seeds**

2 teaspoons **sumac**

2 teaspoons **harissa**

2 tablespoons **red wine vinegar**

1 tablespoon finely chopped **preserved lemon**

4 tablespoons chopped **coriander (cilantro) leaves**

4 tablespoons chopped **mint**

Put the couscous in a bowl, cover with water and leave for 1 minute. Strain, then return the couscous to the bowl and leave for about 5 minutes to swell, stirrring occasionally with a fork to keep the grains separated.

Line a steamer or the top of a couscoussier with two layers of muslin (cheesecloth) or a clean tea towel (dish cloth), then place the couscous in the muslin. Sit the steamer over a saucepan of boiling water and steam, uncovered, for 15 minutes, stirring occasionally with a fork to separate the grains.

Melt the butter in a frying pan over medium heat, add the spring onion, garlic, cumin, sumac, harissa and vinegar and stir-fry for 1 minute. Add the couscous and stir-fry until heated through. Remove from the heat and stir in the preserved lemon, coriander and mint. Season to taste and serve.

tip **Couscous is lighter and fluffier when steamed rather than prepared by other methods. It takes longer but the results are worthwhile. It can be cooked ahead of time, even the day before, and served cold or reheated in the steamer or a microwave oven.**

corn on the cob with chive and lemon butter

serves 4

4 **corn cobs** with husks still on

60 g (2 1/4 oz) **butter**, softened

1 1/2 tablespoons snipped **chives**

1/2 teaspoon grated **lemon zest**

Pull back the husks of the corn cobs, leaving them attached. Remove the silk and trim the top of the cobs.

Combine the butter, chives and lemon zest, season with salt and freshly ground black pepper and spread over the cobs. Pull the husks up again and tie the top of each firmly with string.

Put the cobs in a steamer and cover with a lid. Sit the steamer over a saucepan or wok of boiling water and steam for 10 minutes, or until tender. Remove the husks and serve.

flower rolls with spring onions

makes 12

1 teaspoon **dried yeast**

2 teaspoons **sugar**

350 g (12 oz/2 3/4 cups) **plain (all-purpose) flour**

1/2 teaspoon **baking powder**

1 tablespoon **sesame oil**

1 teaspoon **salt flakes**

6 **spring onions (scallions)**, finely chopped

Sprinkle half the salt over the dough, press it in gently, then **scatter with** half the spring onion.

Press firmly down into the centre, causing the **layers** of dough to open up like **petals**.

Put 200 ml (7 fl oz) of warm water in a bowl and sprinkle the yeast and sugar on top. Leave in a warm spot for about 10 minutes, or until foaming.

Sift in the flour and baking powder and stir with a wooden spoon until the mixture forms a loose dough. Transfer to a lightly floured surface and knead for about 5–6 minutes, or until smooth and elastic (avoid adding extra flour, as a stiff dough will give tough rolls). Shape the dough into a ball.

Spray a large bowl with oil and roll the dough around to coat. Cover the bowl with a clean tea towel (dish towel) and leave in a warm spot for 1 1/2–2 hours, or until the dough doubles in size.

Return the dough to the floured surface and knead for 1 minute. Divide into two portions and cover one with the tea towel. Roll the other out to a thin 30 x 40 cm (12 x 16 inch) rectangle and brush with half the sesame oil. Sprinkle half of the salt over the surface and press it in gently, then scatter with half the spring onion.

Starting at one long end roll the dough up, Swiss-roll (jelly-roll) fashion, then cut into 12 equal slices. Put one slice on top of another, giving six little piles. Using chopsticks, press firmly down into the centre of each pile, causing the layers of dough to open up like the petals of a flower.

Repeat with the remaining dough. Place the rolls on a lightly floured tray, cover with a clean tea towel and leave in a warm spot for 1 hour, or until doubled in size.

Arrange half the rolls in a large oiled steamer and cover with a lid. Sit the steamer over a wok or saucepan of boiling water and steam for 6–8 minutes, or until the rolls are cooked. Repeat with the remaining rolls. Serve warm with Asian dishes.

baby fennel with lemon and anchovy butter

serves 4

4 **baby fennel bulbs**

60 g (2 1/4 oz) **butter**

8 **anchovy fillets**, finely chopped

1 **garlic clove**, crushed

2 small **red chillies**, seeded and finely chopped

2 tablespoons **lemon juice**

Cut the stems off the fennel bulbs, then cut the bulbs lengthways into quarters. Put them in a steamer and cover with a lid. Sit the steamer over a saucepan or wok of simmering water and steam for 5 minutes, or until tender.

Melt the butter in a frying pan over medium heat, add the anchovies, garlic and chilli and cook, stirring, for 30 seconds. Stir in the lemon juice, add the fennel and toss until combined.

witlof with cheese and pecan topping

serves 4

4 **witlof (chicory/Belgian endive)**, large outer leaves removed, then halved
80 g (2 3/4 oz/1 cup) **fresh breadcrumbs**
3 tablespoons grated **parmesan cheese**
3 tablespoons chopped **pecans**
1 tablespoon chopped **thyme**
1 tablespoon snipped **chives**
3 slices of **prosciutto**, roughy chopped
60 g (2 1/4 oz) **butter**, melted

Put the witlof halves in a large steamer and cover with a lid. Sit the steamer over a saucepan or wok of boiling water and steam for 15 minutes, or until tender (test by inserting a skewer into the thickest part). Transfer to a baking tray, cut side up.

Preheat the oven to 200°C (400°F/Gas 6). Combine the breadcrumbs, cheese, pecans, thyme, chives and prosciutto in a bowl, then stir in the butter. Spoon the mixture over the cut side of the witlof, pressing down lightly. Bake for 10 minutes, or until golden and crunchy.

tip **The witlof can be cooked in advance up until the stage of topping them with the breadcrumb mixture. Refrigerate until needed, then top with the mixture and bake just before serving.**

hot pumpkin with taleggio and herbs

serves 6

1 kg (2 lb 4 oz) **butternut pumpkin (squash)**, cut into 4 cm (1 1/2 inch) cubes
90 g (3 1/4 oz) **taleggio cheese**, finely sliced (see tip)
1 tablespoon chopped **parsley**
1 teaspoon chopped **oregano**
1 teaspoon **thyme**
1 teaspoon freshly grated **nutmeg**

Put the pumpkin in a large steamer and cover with a lid. Sit the steamer over a saucepan or wok of simmering water and steam for 20–25 minutes, or until the pumpkin is tender.

Preheat the oven to 200°C (400°F/Gas 6).

Pile the pumpkin cubes into an ovenproof dish and bake for about 10 minutes to dry out the pumpkin a little. Arrange the cheese on top and bake for a further 3–4 minutes, or until the cheese has melted.

Combine the herbs and nutmeg and sprinkle over the melted cheese. Season well with salt and black pepper and serve immediately.

tip **Taleggio is a strong, salty cheese. If you prefer something a little milder, you can use any melting cheese, such as gruyère, fontina, raclette or even cheddar cheese.**

asian greens with oyster sauce and sesame

serves 4

400 g (14 oz/1 bunch) **baby bok choy (pak choy)**, trimmed

400 g (14 oz/1 bunch) **choy sum**, trimmed

200 g (7 oz/1 bunch) **broccolini**, trimmed

4 tablespoons **oyster sauce**

1 tablespoon **light soy sauce**

1 teaspoon **sesame oil**

2 teaspoons **sesame seeds**, lightly toasted

Cut the bok choy into quarters lengthways, then thoroughly wash and drain. Wash the choy sum and broccolini, drain and cut into 5 cm (2 inch) pieces.

Arrange the broccolini and choy sum stalks in the base of a steamer and put the remaining greens on top. Cover with a lid. Sit the steamer over a wok or saucepan of boiling water and steam for about 5 minutes, or until the vegetables are wilted and just tender.

Meanwhile, put the oyster sauce, soy sauce and sesame oil in a small saucepan and warm over low heat. Pile the steamed vegetables on a serving plate, drizzle the sauce over the top and garnish with the sesame seeds. Serve immediately.

brussels sprouts in mustard butter

serves 4

500 g (1 lb 2 oz) **brussels sprouts**

30 g (1 oz) **butter**

3 teaspoons **wholegrain mustard**

2 teaspoons **honey**

Trim the ends and remove any loose leaves from the brussels sprouts. Make a small slit across the base of the stem. Put the sprouts in a large steamer and cover with a lid. Sit the steamer over a saucepan or wok of boiling water and steam for 15 minutes, or until tender. Refresh under cold water to stop the cooking process.

Put the butter, mustard and honey in a saucepan over low heat and stir to melt the butter. Add the sprouts and toss until well coated in the butter mixture and heated through. Pile onto a serving plate and serve immediately.

quinoa with winter greens

serves 4

200 g (7 oz/1 cup) **quinoa**

250 ml (9 fl oz/1 cup) **chicken** or **vegetable stock**

5 **brussels sprouts**, thickly sliced

100 g (3 1/2 oz/2 cups) shredded **cavolo nero** or **silverbeet (Swiss chard)**

1/2 small **red onion**, finely sliced

25 g (1 oz/1/4 cup) **walnut halves**, broken

dressing

1 1/2 tablespoons **olive oil**

1 tablespoon **walnut oil**

2 teaspoons **balsamic vinegar**

2 teaspoons **dijon mustard**

1 **garlic clove**, crushed

Put the quinoa in a bowl and cover with water. Leave for 2–3 minutes, then strain. Transfer to a large shallow saucepan which has a tight-fitting lid and lightly season with salt. Stir in the stock and scatter the brussels sprouts over the top.

Bring to the boil over medium heat then reduce the heat to low. Cover the pan with a sheet of foil, then the lid, and steam for 10–15 minutes. Add the cavolo nero and turn the quinoa over with a fork. Steam for a further 10 minutes, or until the sprouts are tender and the cavolo nero has wilted.

Meanwhile, to make the dressing, combine the olive oil, walnut oil, vinegar, mustard and garlic in a jar. Cover and shake well, then season to taste with salt and freshly ground black pepper.

Put the onion and walnuts in a large bowl. Transfer the contents of the steamer to the bowl, add the dressing and gently combine using a fork. This dish can be served warm or at room temperature.

spaghettini with tomato sauce en papillote

serves 4 as a side dish or 2 as a main

250 g (9 oz) **spaghettini**
4 slices of **smoked bacon**, rind on
2 **garlic cloves**, crushed
50 g (1 3/4 oz/1/3 cup) pitted **kalamata olives**, chopped
1 handful **basil**, chopped, plus extra leaves to garnish
400 ml (14 fl oz) **tomato juice**
1 large **avocado**, cut into cubes

Preheat the oven to 180°C (350°F/Gas 4) and cut four 40 cm (16 inch) lengths of baking paper.

Cook the spaghettini in a large saucepan of salted boiling water for 2 minutes less than the packet instructions. Drain quickly, allowing some of the cooking water to remain on the pasta. Set aside.

Meanwhile, remove the rind and fat from the bacon and put in a hot frying pan to render the fat. Dice the remaining bacon. Once the fat is rendered, discard the rinds. Cook the bacon in the fat until golden and crispy. Add the garlic and cook for a further 30 seconds. Remove from the heat. Add a quarter of the cooked spaghettini to the pan and mix it around to soak up all the fat from the pan.

Repeat with more spaghetti to clean the pan, then transfer the bacon and all the pasta to a large bowl. Add the olives, basil and half the tomato juice. Season well with salt and black pepper and toss everything together.

Divide the pasta equally among the four pieces of paper (this is easiest done using tongs and twisting the pasta into a neat pile in the centre) and drizzle the remaining tomato juice over the top. Seal the parcels by bringing two sides up over the pasta and folding the edges over, then tuck the ends under. Place on two baking trays and bake for 15 minutes.

Just before serving, scatter with the avocado and extra basil leaves. Serve as an accompaniment to chicken, pork or fish dishes.

tip **These parcels can be prepared to wrapping stage several hours in advance, making them perfect for dinner parties.**

pea and lettuce wraps

serves 4

200 g (7 oz/1 1/3 cups) frozen **peas**

2 **garlic cloves**, crushed

1 1/2 tablespoons **thick (double/heavy) cream**

1 teaspoon **sugar**

2 tablespoons finely chopped **basil**

4 large **iceberg lettuce leaves**

olive oil, to serve

Combine the peas, garlic, cream, sugar and basil in a bowl and season with salt and and freshly ground pepper.

Spoon the mixture into the four lettuce leaves and fold to create parcels. Wrap each of these parcels tightly in a sheet of greased foil and place in a steamer. Cover with a lid. Sit the steamer over a saucepan or wok of boiling water and steam for 8–10 minutes, or until heated through. Carefully remove the parcels from the foil and serve hot with a drizzle of olive oil and a sprinkling of salt and pepper.

stuffed zucchini

serves 4

20 g (3/4 oz) **butter**

1 **leek**, white part only, halved lengthways and finely sliced

2 tablespoons **pine nuts**

1 tablespoon shredded **basil**

4 tablespoons **crème fraîche** or **sour cream**

50 g (1 3/4 oz/1/4 cup) cooked **wild rice/long-grain rice blend** (see tip)

pinch of freshly grated **nutmeg**

2 **zucchini (courgettes)**

Heat the butter in a small frying pan over low heat. Add the leek and cook without browning for 2–3 minutes. Stir in the pine nuts, basil, crème fraîche and rice, and cook for 5 minutes. If the mixture becomes dry, add a little hot water. Add the nutmeg and season well with salt and freshly ground black pepper.

Halve the zucchini lengthways and scoop out the seeds using a teaspoon or melon baller. Season lightly with salt then spoon the filling into the cavities, piling it up.

Arrange the zucchini in a large steamer and cover with a lid. Sit the steamer over a saucepan or wok of boiling water and simmer for 6–8 minutes, or until tender. Serve immediately.

tip **You will need to cook 25 g (1 oz) of uncooked wild rice in boiling water for about 30 minutes to get this quantity.**

syrian burghul

serves 4

2 tablespoons **olive oil**

1 large **onion**, finely chopped

1/2 teaspoon **dried mint**

175 g (6 oz/1 cup) coarse **burghul (bulgur)**

500 ml (17 fl oz/2 cups) **chicken** or **vegetable stock**

70 g (2 1/2 oz/1 cup) shredded **red cabbage**

2 tablespoons chopped **parsley**

1 small handful **mint**, roughly torn

40 g (1 1/2 oz/1/4 cup) pitted **kalamata olives**, halved

1/2 **lemon**

1/2 **pomegranate**

200 g (7 oz/heaped 3/4 cup) **Greek-style yoghurt**

Heat the oil in a large deep frying pan with a tight-fitting lid over medium heat. Add the onion and dried mint and cook for 5 minutes, or until the onion is soft. Stir in the bulgur until coated, then add the stock. Cover with the lid and steam over low heat for 30 minutes. Do not remove the lid during this time.

Stir with a fork, lifting up any crunchy bits from the bottom of the pan. Add the cabbage, parsley, fresh mint and olives. Finely grate the lemon zest and add to the pan, then squeeze in the lemon juice. Holding the pomegranate over the pan to catch the juice, scoop the seeds into the pan. Squeeze any remaining juice into the pan and discard any white pith that may have dropped in. Season with salt and freshly ground black pepper and toss lightly. Serve warm with the yoghurt.

creamy celeriac parcels

serves 4

125 ml (4 fl oz/1/2 cup) **dry white wine**

125 ml (4 fl oz/1/2 cup) **cream (whipping)**

1 teaspoon **ground cumin**

1 tablespoon **wholegrain mustard**

1 **celeriac**, weighing about 600 g (1 lb 5 oz), peeled and finely sliced, then cut into julienne strips

Preheat the oven to 180°C (350°F/Gas 4). Combine the wine, cream, cumin and mustard in a bowl and season well with salt and freshly ground black pepper. Add the celeriac and toss well to coat. Leave for a couple of minutes.

Meanwhile, cut four 50 cm (20 inch) lengths of baking paper. Divide the mixture into four and place it in the middle of each piece (it's easiest to do this using your hands). Spoon any remaining cream mixture over the top. Seal the parcels by bringing the two long sides up over the celeriac and folding the edges over a few times. Then twist the ends tightly together and tuck the ends under. It's important that the packages are sealed tightly, otherwise the celeriac won't steam properly.

Put the parcels on one or two baking trays and bake for 45 minutes, or until the celeriac is tender. Leave to cool slightly for a couple of minutes before opening. Delicious served with roast meats.

steamed vegetables with horseradish butter

serves 4

1 tablespoon **creamed horseradish**

30 g (1 oz) **butter**, softened

1 tablespoon finely chopped **chervil**

24 **baby carrots**, scrubbed, topped and tailed, and any large ones halved lengthways

200 g (7 oz) **green beans**, trimmed and halved on the diagonal

2 **zucchini (courgettes)**, cut into batons

Combine the horseradish with the butter and chervil in a small bowl and season with salt and freshly ground black pepper. Cover and refrigerate to harden slightly.

Line a steamer with baking paper and punch with holes. Add the carrots and cover with a lid. Sit the steamer over a saucepan or wok of boiling water and steam for 6 minutes. Add the beans and zucchini and steam for a further 6 minutes, or until all the vegetables are tender but still slightly crunchy. Transfer to a sieve to drain off any water.

Arrange the vegetables on a warmed serving dish and dot the horseradish butter on top. Mix the vegetables around to melt the butter slightly, then serve.

cauliflower with watercress dressing

serves 4–6

1/2 large **cauliflower**, chopped into florets

90 g (3 1/4 oz/3 cups) **watercress**, leaves only

1 large handful **parsley**, roughly chopped

2 **garlic cloves**, chopped

2 teaspoons **lemon juice**

125 g (4 1/2 oz/1/2 cup) **whole-egg mayonnaise**

40 g (1 1/2 oz/1/4 cup) **pine nuts**, toasted

Line a steamer with baking paper and punch with holes. Lay the cauliflower florets in a single layer on top and cover with a lid. Sit the steamer over a saucepan or wok of boiling water and steam for 12–15 minutes, or until tender.

Meanwhile, blanch the watercress in boiling water. Drain well. Put the watercress, parsley, garlic and lemon juice in a food processor and blend until roughly chopped. Add the mayonnaise and pulse to combine.

Arrange the hot cauliflower on a serving dish and drizzle the watercress dressing over the top. Garnish with pine nuts and serve hot or cold.

smoked cod kedgeree

serves 6

350 g (12 oz) **smoked cod fillets**
30 g (1 oz) **butter**
1 tablespoon **mustard oil** or **olive oil**
1 **onion**, finely chopped
2 x 3 cm (3/4 x 1 1/4 inch) piece **ginger**, grated
2 **garlic cloves**, crushed
1 1/2 tablespoons medium **curry powder**
900 g (2 lb/5 cups) steamed **basmati rice** (see tip)
100 g (3 1/2 oz/2/3 cup) frozen **peas**
2 tablespoons **lemon juice**
1 handful **coriander (cilantro) leaves**, chopped
1 handful **flat-leaf (Italian) parsley**, chopped
3 **eggs**, hard-boiled
2 tablespoons **fried shallots** (see tip)

Line a steamer with foil and punch with holes. Place the cod fillets in a single layer on top and cover with a lid. Sit the steamer over a saucepan or wok of boiling water and steam for 8–10 minutes, or until the fish is cooked through. Set aside to cool, then remove the bones and skin and flake the flesh.

Heat the butter and oil in a large frying pan over medium heat, add the onion, ginger and garlic and cook, stirring, for 2 minutes, or until the onion is soft. Add the curry powder and stir for 2 minutes, or until fragrant.

Add the rice to the pan and stir gently until the grains are separated. Stir in the peas and cook until the rice is heated through and is well coated. Add the cod, lemon juice, coriander and parsley and mix well. Season with salt and pepper. Garnish with the hard-boiled eggs and fried shallots and serve immediately.

tips **Kedgeree also makes a delicious light supper or weekend breakfast. You will need 600 g (1 lb 5 oz/3 cups) of uncooked rice to make this quantity of cooked rice. Fried shallots are deep-fried red Asian shallots and they are usually used as a garnish, to add crunch and flavour. Look for them in the Asian section of large supermarkets or in Asian grocery stores.**

Steam the **cod fillets**, then remove the bones and skin and **flake** the flesh.

Add the **curry** powder to the onion mixture and stir until **fragrant**.

ratatouille parcels with aïoli

serves 4

1 **garlic bulb**, left whole

4 long, thin **eggplants (aubergines)**, quartered lengthways

4 small **white zucchini (courgettes)**, quartered lengthways

4 **baby carrots**, trimmed

2 **bulb spring onions (scallions)**, quartered

250 g (9 oz) **baby roma (plum) tomatoes**, halved

3 tablespoons **olive oil**

1 teaspoon **dried oregano**

125 g (4 1/2 oz/1/2 cup) **whole-egg mayonnaise**

Line a steamer with baking paper and punch with holes. Place the garlic bulb on top and cover with a lid. Sit the steamer over a saucepan or wok of boiling water and steam for 35 minutes, or until the garlic is soft. Set aside to cool.

Lay four 60 cm (24 inch) pieces of baking paper on a flat surface. Arrange four pieces of eggplant and zucchini, a carrot, two pieces of spring onion and a few tomato halves in the centre of each piece. Drizzle with oil, top with a little oregano and season with salt and pepper. Fold the paper over the vegetables to form a parcel, making sure the ends are folded and pressed down well to prevent leakage. Place the ratatouille parcels in a single layer in the steamer, then cover and steam over boiling water for 12 minutes.

Meanwhile, to make the aïoli cut the top off the garlic bulb and gently squeeze the flesh into a small bowl. Mash lightly with a fork, then stir in the mayonnaise.

To serve, open each parcel and top with a good dollop of aïoli.

herb pilaff

serves 6

40 g (1 1/2 oz) **butter**

1 small **onion**, grated

400 g (14 oz/2 cups) **basmati rice**

875 ml (30 fl oz/3 1/2 cups) **chicken stock**

2 **bay leaves**

3 tablespoons chopped **flat-leaf (Italian) parsley**

3 tablespoons chopped **coriander (cilantro) leaves**

Heat the butter in a saucepan over medium heat, add the onion and cook, stirring, for 4 minutes, or until soft. Stir in the rice, mixing well to coat in the butter. Add the stock and bay leaves, bring to the boil, then reduce the heat to low and cover with a tight-fitting lid. Steam for 15–20 minutes, or until all the liquid has been absorbed.

Leave to rest for 5 minutes, then remove the bay leaves and season with salt and freshly ground black pepper. Add the parsley and coriander, stir it through with a fork and serve.

cauliflower with pancetta and caramelized onions

serves 4–6

50 g (1 3/4 oz) **butter**

2 **onions**, finely sliced

1 **bay leaf**

2 **garlic cloves**, finely chopped

1/4 teaspoon freshly grated **nutmeg**

40 g (1 1/2 oz/1/4 cup) **pine nuts**

2 tablespoons finely chopped **parsley**

6 slices of **pancetta**

500 g (1 lb 2 oz) **cauliflower**, chopped into small florets

Melt the butter in a large frying pan over medium heat. Add the onion and bay leaf, season generously with salt and freshly ground black pepper and cook, stirring occasionally, for 30 minutes, or until the onion is dark brown and caramelized. Add the garlic, nutmeg and pine nuts to the pan and cook for a further 5 minutes, then toss in the parsley. Remove from the heat.

Meanwhile, preheat a grill (broiler) to high and cook the pancetta for 3 minutes each side, or until crisp and golden. Remove from the heat and allow to cool, then break it up into smaller pieces.

Line a large steamer with baking paper and punch with holes. Place the cauliflower on top and cover with a lid. Sit the steamer over a saucepan or wok of boiling water and steam for 5–6 minutes, or until tender.

Arrange the cauliflower on a serving plate, spoon the onion and pine nut mixture over the top and sprinkle with the pancetta. Serve immediately.

broad bean and pea pesto with broccolini

serves 4

100 g (3 1/2 oz/2/3 cup) frozen **peas**

115 g (4 oz/3/4 cup) frozen shelled **broad (fava) beans**

35 g (1 1/4 oz/1/3 cup) grated **parmesan cheese**

4 tablespoons finely chopped **basil**

1 **garlic clove**, crushed

2 teaspoons grated **lemon zest**

30 g (1 oz/1/4 cup) roughly chopped toasted **pecans**

4 tablespoons **olive oil**

425 g (15 oz/2 bunches) **broccolini**, washed and stems trimmed

Steam the peas and **broad beans** until they are only half cooked.

Add the parmesan, basil, garlic and **lemon zest**, season with salt and pepper and **pulse** briefly.

Place the peas and broad beans in a steamer and cover with a lid. Sit the steamer over a saucepan or wok of boiling water and steam for 2 minutes, or until the peas and beans are only half cooked.

Strain the peas and beans into a colander, then refresh under cold running water. Drain well, then put them in a food processor. Add the parmesan, basil, garlic, lemon zest and salt and freshly ground pepper, and pulse briefly so that the mixture isn't overly processed (it should be quite rough). Spoon the mixture into a large bowl, add the pecans and stir in the olive oil. Check the seasoning and add more salt and pepper if necessary.

Put the broccolini in a steamer and cover with a lid. Steam for 5 minutes, or until the broccolini is a little under-cooked.

Stir 2 tablespoons of the steaming water into the pesto, then add the hot broccolini and carefully toss through. Serve immediately.

asparagus bundles

serves 4

12 **asparagus spears**

1 tablespoon **extra virgin olive oil**

1 tablespoon **lemon juice**

4 slices of **prosciutto**

60 g (2 1/4 oz/1/4 cup) **ricotta cheese**

25 g (1 oz/1/4 cup) grated **parmesan cheese**

Break the ends off the asparagus spears and cut the spears in half crossways. Place in a steamer and cover with a lid. Sit the steamer over a saucepan or wok of boiling water and steam for 5–7 minutes, or until tender.

Transfer the asparagus to a small bowl and toss with the olive oil, lemon juice and some salt and pepper. Wrap bundles of six asparagus pieces (three of each end) in each slice of prosciutto and place on a grill (broiler) tray.

Mix together the ricotta and parmesan and spread the mixture over the prosciutto. Place the tray under a preheated medium grill for 10 minutes, or until the cheese starts to turn golden. Serve immediately.

warm potatoes and broad beans

serves 4

8 **new potatoes**, halved or quartered if large

235 g (8 1/2 oz/1 1/2 cups) fresh or frozen **broad (fava) beans**, shelled (see tip)

1 **spring onion (scallion)**, finely sliced

2 tablespoons **extra virgin olive oil**

1 tablespoon **red wine vinegar**

1–2 tablespoons **baby capers**, rinsed and squeezed dry

1 small handful **flat-leaf (Italian) parsley**, roughly chopped

Put the potatoes in a steamer and cover with a lid. Sit the steamer over a saucepan or wok of boiling water and steam for 10 minutes, or until tender. Transfer to a bowl and cover with foil.

Place the broad beans in the steamer and steam, covered, for 5 minutes, or until tender. Add to the bowl of potatoes, along with the spring onion, oil, vinegar, capers and parsley. Toss gently to combine and serve.

tip **Broad beans don't have to be skinned but if you prefer them skinned, steam them until tender, then rinse under cold water until they are just cool enough to handle. Hold each bean at the stem end, pinch the other end to break the skin and squeeze out the bean.**

parcels of snake beans with spiced peanuts

serves 6

spiced peanuts

80 g (2 3/4 oz/1/2 cup) toasted **peanuts**

1 **garlic clove**, finely chopped

1 tablespoon grated fresh **ginger**

1/2 teaspoon **ground fennel**

1 large **red chilli**, seeded and finely chopped

1 tablespoon grated **palm sugar** or **soft brown sugar**

1 tablespoon **peanut oil**

1 tablespoon **lime juice**

3 tablespoons **fried shallots**

2 tablespoons finely chopped **coriander (cilantro) leaves**

320 g (11 1/4 oz) **snake (yard-long) beans**, cut into 8 cm (3 1/4 inch) lengths

2 teaspoons **sesame oil**

12 **garlic chives**

Put the peanuts, garlic, ginger, ground fennel, chilli, palm sugar and 1/2 teaspoon of salt in a food processor. Process until it reaches a coarse texture. Heat the oil in a frying pan over medium–high heat. Add the peanut mixture and cook, stirring well, for 2–3 minutes, or until lightly brown and fragrant. Add the lime juice and fried shallots and cook for a further minute. Remove from the heat and set aside to cool. When the mixture has cooled a little, toss in the chopped coriander.

Meanwhile, put the snake beans in a steamer and cover with a lid. Sit the steamer over a wok or saucepan of boiling water and steam for 5 minutes, or until the beans are tender, then remove and set aside to cool a little. When the beans are cool enough to handle, toss with the sesame oil.

Bundle the beans into 12 even-sized parcels and tie together with a garlic chive. Place the beans on a serving platter and spoon the spiced peanuts over the top. Serve immediately.

comforting cheesy mash

serves 4

900 g (2 lb) **roasting (floury) potatoes**, cut into even-sized pieces
2 **garlic cloves**, crushed
125 ml (4 fl oz/1/2 cup) **milk**
125 g (41/2 oz/1 cup) grated **gruyère** or **cheddar cheese**

Put the potatoes in a steamer and cover with a lid. Sit the steamer over a saucepan or wok of boiling water and steam for 20–30 minutes, or until tender.

Transfer the potato to a bowl and add the garlic and milk. Mash with a potato masher, then beat until fluffy. Season to taste with salt and freshly ground pepper. Stir in the cheese and beat again until the cheese has melted.

desserts

oranges in spiced syrup

serves 4

4 **oranges**, peeled and sliced widthways into 1 cm (1/2 inch) thick slices
185 g (6 1/2 oz/3/4 cup) **Greek-style yoghurt**
3 tablespoons **thick (double/heavy) cream**
1 teaspoon **honey**

syrup
115 g (4 oz/1/2 cup) grated **palm sugar** or **soft brown sugar**
1 **star anise**
2 **vanilla beans**, split, seeds scraped
1 **cinnamon stick**
1 tablespoon **orange blossom water** (see tip)
zest of 1 **orange**, peeled in thick strips

Arrange the orange slices on a plate that fits into a large steamer, then put the plate in the steamer and cover with a lid. Sit the steamer over a saucepan or wok of boiling water and steam for 5–8 minutes, or until the oranges are warm and have started to release some of their juices. Carefully remove the plate from the steamer. Using a spatula, lift the orange slices into a bowl and reserve the orange liquid.

To make the syrup, put the sugar and 185 ml (6 fl oz/3/4 cup) of water in a small saucepan over medium–high heat and stir until the sugar has dissolved. Add the star anise, vanilla beans and seeds, cinnamon stick, orange blossom water, orange zest and reserved orange liquid and simmer for 10 minutes, or until the liquid has reduced by half. Pour the syrup over the oranges and leave to cool completely. Refrigerate for 1 hour to chill.

When you are ready to serve, mix together the yoghurt, cream and honey. Put three or four slices of orange on individual serving plates and top with a vanilla bean half and some orange zest. Drizzle with some of the syrup and serve with a generous dollop of honey yoghurt.

tip **Orange blossom water is used in a many Middle Eastern desserts. It is available from health food shops and delicatessens, and can sometimes be found in the cake-making section of larger supermarkets.**

passionfruit cream sponge roll

serves 8

4 **eggs**, separated
175 g (6 oz/3/4 cup) **caster (superfine) sugar**
1 teaspoon **natural vanilla extract**
90 g (3 1/4 oz/3/4 cup) **cornflour (cornstarch)**
3 tablespoons **plain (all-purpose) flour**
1 1/2 teaspoons **baking powder**
boiling **water**, for steaming
2 tablespoons **icing (confectioners') sugar**, for dusting

passionfruit cream

310 ml (10 3/4 fl oz/1 1/4 cups) **cream (whipping)**, whipped
3 tablespoons **icing (confectioners') sugar**, sifted
2 tablespoons **passionfruit pulp** (about 2 passionfruit)

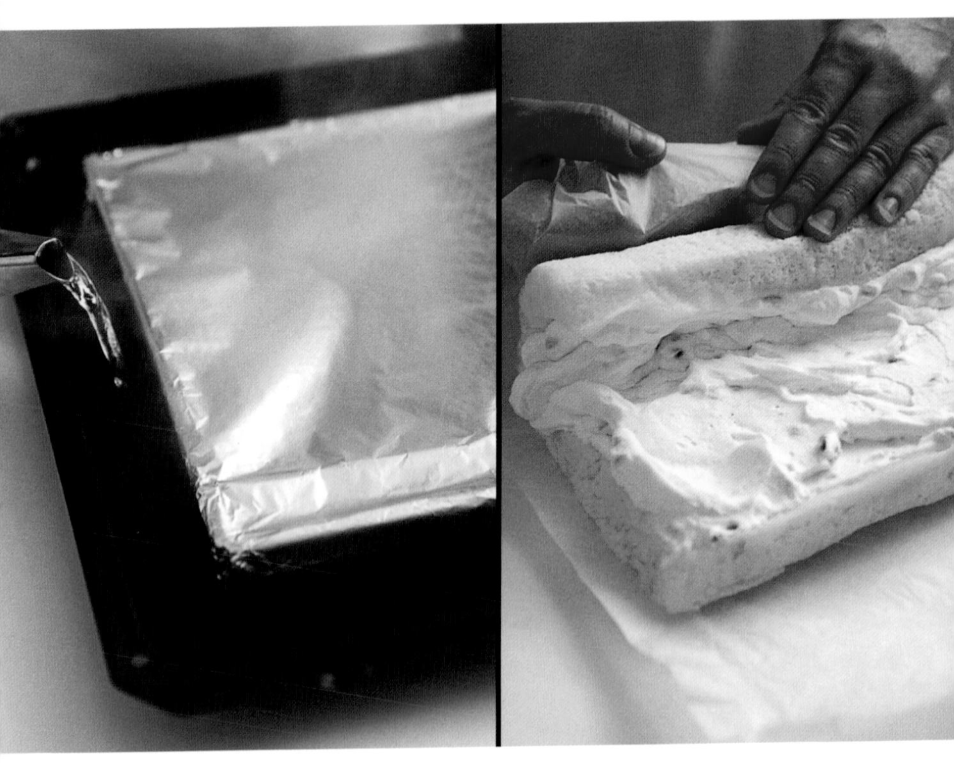

Put the tin in a large deep roasting tin and pour in **boiling water** to come halfway up the sides of the **Swiss roll** tin.

Using the baking paper as a guide, **gently** roll the cake into a **log**.

Preheat the oven to 180°C (350°F/Gas 4) and line a 29 x 24 x 3 cm (11 1/2 x 9 1/2 x 1 1/4 inch) Swiss roll tin (jelly roll tin) with baking paper.

Using electric beaters, beat the egg whites and a pinch of salt until soft peaks form. Gradually beat in the sugar until the mixture is thick and glossy. Add the egg yolks and vanilla extract, and beat until well combined.

In a separate bowl, mix together the cornflour, plain flour and baking powder. Sift the flours twice, then carefully fold into the egg mixture. Don't over-stir as the cake will lose its light texture.

Pour the mixture into the prepared tin and smooth with a spatula. Cover with foil, then place the tin in a large deep roasting tin and pour in enough boiling water to come halfway up the sides of the Swiss roll tin. Bake for 35–45 minutes, or until golden and springy to the touch. Cool in the tin for 1 minute, then run a knife around the edges of the tin to loosen the sponge cake. Place a large piece of baking paper on a clean surface. Invert the cake onto the baking paper then gently peel away the baking paper from the bottom of the cake. Using the baking paper as a guide, gently roll the cake into a log, starting from the long side. This needs to be done while the cake is still hot to prevent cracking. Leave to cool for 20 minutes.

Meanwhile, to make the passionfruit cream, whip the cream and icing sugar until stiff, then fold in the passionfruit pulp. Gently unroll the cake and spread with the passionfruit cream. Re-roll, then dust with icing sugar and serve at once. This is best eaten on the day it is made.

sticky fig and hazelnut puddings

makes 6

70 g (2 1/2 oz/1/2 cup) toasted **hazelnuts**
150 ml (5 fl oz) fresh **orange juice**
100 g (3 1/2 oz/1/2 cup) chopped **dried figs**, plus 6 dried figs, extra, cut horizontally
1/4 teaspoon **ground ginger**
1/4 teaspoon **ground cinnamon**
3 teaspoons finely grated **orange zest**
1/2 teaspoon **bicarbonate of soda (baking soda)**
80 g (2 3/4 oz) **butter**, softened
115 g (4 oz/1/2 cup) **soft brown sugar**
1 **egg**
90 g (3 1/4 oz/3/4 cup) **self-raising flour**
2 tablespoons **maple syrup**
boiling **water**, for steaming
thick (double/heavy) cream, to serve

Preheat the oven to 200°C (400°F/Gas 6). Spread the hazelnuts out on a tray and place in the oven for 10–15 minutes. Tip the nuts onto a clean tea towel (dish towel) and gently rub to remove the skins. Put the nuts in a food processor and pulse until finely ground. Grease six 250 ml (9 fl oz/1 cup) ramekins or ovenproof teacups and place a square of baking paper in the base of each.

Pour the orange juice into a saucepan and bring to the boil over medium heat. Add the chopped figs, ginger, cinnamon and 1 teaspoon of the orange zest and cook for 1 minute. Remove from the heat and add the bicarbonate of soda (allowing the mixture to froth), then set aside to cool for 10 minutes.

Meanwhile, combine the butter and sugar in a large bowl and beat with electric beaters until light and fluffy. Add the egg and beat until well combined. Fold in the hazelnuts, and add the flour in three batches, incorporating each batch well into the mixture before adding the next (the mixture will become stiff). Pour the orange sauce into the pudding mixture and stir well to combine.

Pour the maple syrup into the base of the ramekins and top with the remaining orange zest. Arrange two of the extra fig halves in the base of each ramekin. Spoon in the pudding mixture until it is three-quarters full, then cover each ramekin securely with a square sheet of foil. Arrange the puddings in the base of a deep roasting tin. Fill the baking tin with enough boiling water to come halfway up the sides of the ramekins, and bake the puddings for 35 minutes, or until cooked. Set the ramekins aside for 5 minutes before inverting onto a plate and serving with cream.

lemon and lime curds

makes 6

4 **eggs**

2 **egg yolks**

175 g (6 oz/3/4 cup) **caster (superfine) sugar**

100 ml (3 1/2 fl oz) **lemon juice**

2 1/2 tablespoons **lime juice**

finely grated zest of 2 **limes**

300 ml (10 1/2 fl oz) **cream (whipping)**

boiling **water**, for steaming

baby meringues, to serve

thick (double/heavy) cream, to serve

candied lemons

115 g (4 oz/1/2 cup) **caster (superfine) sugar**

1 **lemon**, finely sliced

Preheat the oven to 160°C (315°F/Gas 2–3). Line a roasting tin with a tea towel (dish towel), then place six 185 ml (6 fl oz/3/4 cup) ramekins in the tin.

Combine the eggs, egg yolks and sugar in a large bowl and whisk until the sugar has dissolved and the mixture is well combined. Stir in the lemon and lime juice and the lime zest. Add the cream and mix well to combine. Pour the mixture into the ramekins, then pour enough boiling water into the roasting tin to come halfway up the side of the ramekins. Bake for 30 minutes, or until just set (the curds should be slightly wobbly when you shake them). Remove the ramekins from the roasting tin and allow to cool, then refrigerate until cold.

Meanwhile, to make the candied lemons, put the sugar and 125 ml (4 fl oz/1/2 cup) of water in a saucepan over medium–high heat and stir until the sugar has dissolved. Add the lemon slices and bring to the boil. Reduce the heat to medium and simmer without stirring for 5–10 minutes, or until the syrup has reduced a little. Remove from the heat and allow to cool. Chill in the refrigerator until ready to serve.

Place a candied lemon slice on top of each curd and drizzle with some of the syrup. Serve with baby meringues and thick cream.

banana and pear parcels with passionfruit sauce

serves 4

20 g (3/4 oz) **butter**

2 tablespoons **maple syrup**

4 **bananas**, cut into large chunks

3 ripe **pears**, peeled, quartered and cored

vanilla ice cream, to serve (optional)

passionfruit sauce

4 large **passionfruit**

2 tablespoons **soft brown sugar**

Preheat the oven to 180°C (350°F/Gas 4). Cut out four 30 cm (12 inch) squares of baking paper.

Melt the butter and maple syrup in a small saucepan over low heat. Divide the banana chunks and pear quarters among the paper squares, then spoon the maple butter mixture over the top.

For each parcel, bring two paper edges up to the centre and pleat. Pleat the sides to form a secure parcel. Put the parcels on a baking tray and bake for 10 minutes, or until the bananas are softened but still firm.

Meanwhile, to make the passionfruit sauce, combine the passionfruit pulp and sugar and stir until dissolved.

To serve, remove the fruit and sauce from the paper cases and arrange on serving plates. Drizzle with the sauce and serve with a scoop of ice cream, if desired.

orange and almond poppy seed cakes with orange syrup sauce

makes 4

1 **orange**

100 g (3 1/2 oz/1 cup) **ground almonds**

80 g (2 3/4 oz/1/3 cup) **caster (superfine) sugar**

1 tablespoon **poppy seeds**

1 teaspoon **baking powder**

2 **eggs**, lightly beaten

cream or **ice cream**, to serve

orange sauce

thin strips of zest from 1 **orange**

4 tablespoons fresh **orange juice**

55 g (2 oz/1/4 cup) **caster (superfine) sugar**

2 tablespoons chunky **orange marmalade**

Put the orange in a saucepan with enough water to cover. Bring to the boil, then reduce the heat and simmer for about 45 minutes, ensuring the orange stays covered with water. Drain, refresh under cold water, then leave to cool. Cut into quarters and remove the pips. Put the skin and flesh in a food processor and process until smooth.

Preheat the oven to 180°C (350°F/Gas 4). Grease and line the bases of four giant muffin holes with baking paper. Put an ovenproof dish in the oven and half-fill with hot water.

In a large bowl combine the ground almonds, sugar, poppy seeds and baking powder, then stir in the egg and orange purée. Pour into the prepared muffin holes and smooth the surfaces. Cover with a sheet of well-greased baking paper.

Put the muffin tin in the ovenproof dish and bake for 30 minutes, or until the cakes are firm to the touch and come away from the sides a little. Remove from the oven and leave for 5 minutes before turning out of the tin. Peel away the paper.

Meanwhile, to make the orange sauce, put the orange zest, juice and sugar in a saucepan over low heat and stir until the sugar has dissolved. Stir in the marmalade, increase the heat and boil for 5 minutes, or until thick and syrupy.

Serve the cakes face down, topped with the orange sauce and a little cream or ice cream. These are delicious warm or at room temperature.

Put the **orange** skin and flesh in a food processor and process until **smooth**.

Stir in the **marmalade** and boil until the sauce is **thick** and **syrupy**.

warm dried fruit salad with honey yoghurt

serves 4

400 g (14 oz) assorted **dried fruit**, such as prunes, apples, apricots and pears
1 **cinnamon stick**, broken in half
30 g (1 oz/1/3 cup) **flaked almonds**, toasted

honey yoghurt

200 g (7 oz/heaped 3/4 cup) **Greek-style yoghurt**
2 tablespoons **honey**
2 teaspoons **rose water**

Put the dried fruit and cinnamon stick on a plate large enough to just fit into a large steamer. Put the plate in the steamer and cover with a lid. Sit the steamer over a saucepan or wok of boiling water and steam for 20–25 minutes, or until the fruit is nice and plump.

To make the honey yoghurt, combine the yoghurt, honey and rose water in a bowl.

To serve, divide the fruit among four serving bowls and scatter the almonds over the top. Serve with the honey yoghurt.

sticky rice with mango

serves 4

400 g (14 oz/2 cups) **glutinous white rice** (see tip)

250 ml (9 fl oz/1 cup) **coconut milk**

60 g (2 1/4 oz/1/3 cup) grated **palm sugar** or **soft brown sugar**

4 **makrut (kaffir lime) leaves**, crushed

1 **lemon grass stem**, bruised

2 **mangoes**

2 teaspoons grated **palm sugar** or **soft brown sugar**, extra

1 **lime**, quartered

Cook the **rice** in a steamer lined with baking paper until **tender**.

Pour the **coconut** mixture over the rice, **fluffing it up** with a fork as you pour.

Wash the rice under cold running water until the water runs clear. Put it in a bowl, cover with cold water and leave overnight. Drain.

Line a large steamer with baking paper and punch with holes. Put the rice on top and cover with a lid. Sit the steamer over a wok or saucepan of boiling water and steam until the rice is soft (this will take 30–60 minutes, depending on the size of your steamer).

Meanwhile, put the coconut milk, palm sugar, lime leaves and lemon grass in a small saucepan and stir over low heat until the sugar has dissolved. Bring to a simmer and cook for 5 minutes, or until thickened.

Transfer the soft rice to a large bowl and pour the coconut mixture over the top, fluffing the rice with a fork as you pour to coat the rice evenly. Do not stir or the rice will become gluggy. Cover and leave for 10 minutes to absorb the liquid, then remove the lemon grass and lime leaves.

Cut the cheeks from the mangoes to give four cheeks. Cut through the mango flesh in a lattice pattern, taking care not to cut through the skin, and push the skin up to expose the flesh. Sprinkle with the extra palm sugar and serve with the sticky rice and a wedge of lime.

tip **Glutinous rice is also known as sticky rice and is used in both sweet and savoury Asian dishes. It needs overnight soaking prior to cooking. If you don't have time, you can soak the rice for half the time but you will need to increase the cooking time by up to 30 minutes.**

little cherry custards

makes 6

250 ml (9 fl oz/1 cup) **milk**

125 ml (4 fl oz/1/2 cup) **cream (whipping)**

1 **vanilla bean**, split, seeds scraped

1 **cinnamon stick**, broken in half

3 **eggs**

2 **egg yolks**

140 g (5 oz/2/3 cup) **caster (superfine) sugar**

425 g (15 oz) tin stoneless **cherries**, drained, liquid reserved

115 g (4 oz/1/2 cup) **caster (superfine) sugar**, extra

3 tablespoons **kirsch**

Preheat the oven to 160°C (315°F/Gas 2–3) and lightly grease six 125 ml (4 fl oz/1/2 cup) dariole moulds.

Combine the milk and cream in a saucepan. Add the vanilla bean and seeds and the cinnamon stick and heat until almost at boiling point. Remove from the heat.

Put the eggs, egg yolks and sugar in a bowl and whisk to combine. Gradually whisk the hot milk and cream into the egg mixture, then strain into a clean bowl.

Place two or three cherries in the base of each mould and fill with the custard mixture. Sit the custards in a roasting tin and pour in enough hot water to come halfway up the sides of the moulds. Cover with foil, pressing around the edges to form a seal, and steam in the oven for 45–50 minutes, or until a skewer comes out clean when inserted in the middle. Remove from the roasting tin and leave the custards to settle for 3 minutes before inverting onto serving plates.

Meanwhile, put the reserved cherry liquid, extra sugar and kirsch in a heavy-based frying pan over low heat and stir until the sugar has dissolved. Add the remaining cherries, increase the heat and bring to the boil, then reduce the heat and simmer for 15 minutes, or until the liquid becomes syrupy. Spoon the cherry compote over the custards before serving.

ginger nut and lime cheesecake pots

makes 6

6 **ginger nut biscuits (ginger snaps)**

300 ml (10 1/2 fl oz) **thickened (whipping) cream**

250 g (9 oz/1 cup) **cream cheese**, softened

2 **eggs**

80 g (2 3/4 oz/1/3 cup) **caster (superfine) sugar**

2 teaspoons grated **lime zest**

4 tablespoons **lime juice**

Preheat the oven to 160°C (315°F/Gas 2–3). Place a biscuit in the base of six 170 ml (5 1/2 fl oz/2/3 cup) ramekins.

Combine the cream, cream cheese, eggs, sugar, lime zest and juice in a food processor and blend until smooth. Pour the mixture over the biscuits.

Put the ramekins in an ovenproof dish and pour in enough water to come a third of the way up the sides of the ramekins. Bake for 50 minutes, or until just firm in the centre and beginning to brown. Remove the cheesecakes from the ovenproof dish and cool to room temperature before serving.

tip **This dessert is best served at room temperature (without any refrigeration) as this will keep the biscuits crisp. However, if you need to cook them well in advance they can be refrigerated then returned to room temperature before serving.**

carrot and ginger syrup pudding

serves 6

60 g (2 1/4 oz) **unsalted butter**, softened

55 g (2 oz/1/4 cup) **soft brown sugar**

55 g (2 oz/1/4 cup) **caster (superfine) sugar**

2 **eggs**

4 tablespoons **milk**

80 g (2 3/4 oz/1/2 cup) grated **carrot**

2 tablespoons finely chopped **glacé ginger**

90 g (3 1/4 oz/3/4 cup) **self-raising flour**

1/2 teaspoon **bicarbonate of soda (baking soda)**

1/2 teaspoon **mixed spice**

2 tablespoons **golden syrup** or **maple syrup**

cream, ice cream or **custard**, to serve

Press a large piece of baking paper over the base and into the corners of a 20 cm (8 inch) steamer. Pleat the paper up the sides and allow the paper to overlap the top edges. Spray or brush with olive oil.

Using electric beaters, beat the butter, brown sugar and caster sugar in a large bowl until thick and creamy, scraping down the sides of the bowl as you go. Beat in the eggs one at a time. Stir in the milk, carrot and ginger, then add the sifted flour, bicarbonate of soda and mixed spice and stir lightly until combined.

Pour the mixture into the steamer and cover with a lid. Sit the steamer over a saucepan or wok of boiling water and steam for 30 minutes, or until the pudding is firm in the centre. Lift out and drizzle the golden syrup over the top. Cut into wedges and serve hot or at room temperature with cream, ice cream or custard.

spiced tropical fruit pudding

makes 2; each pudding serves 10

750 g (1 lb 10 oz) **dried mixed fruit**
50 g (1 3/4 oz) **dried mangoes**, finely chopped
50 g (1 3/4 oz) **dried peaches**, finely chopped
50 g (1 3/4 oz) **sun-dried bananas**, finely chopped
50 g (1 3/4 oz) **dried figs**, finely chopped
110 g (3 3/4 oz/1/2 cup) **glacé ginger**, chopped
1 **granny smith apple**, peeled and grated
1 tablespoon grated **orange zest**
1 tablespoon grated **lime zest**
110 g (3 3/4 oz/2/3 cup) unsalted **macadamia nuts**, chopped
250 ml (9 fl oz/1 cup) **stout beer**
2 1/2 tablespoons **dark rum**
210 g (7 1/2 oz/1 3/4 cups) **self-raising flour**
1 teaspoon freshly grated **nutmeg**
1 1/2 teaspoons **ground cinnamon**
1 1/2 teaspoons **mixed spice**
250 g (9 oz/heaped 3 cups) **fresh breadcrumbs**
500 g (1 lb 2 oz/2 1/4 cups) **dark brown sugar**
250 g (9 oz) **butter**
4 **eggs**, lightly beaten
custard, to serve

Put all the dried fruit, glacé ginger, apple, orange and lime zest and nuts in a large ceramic bowl. Pour on the beer and rum, cover with plastic wrap and leave to soak overnight in the refrigerator, stirring once or twice.

Sift the flour and spices into a large bowl, then stir in the breadcrumbs and sugar.

Melt the butter in a small saucepan and whisk in the eggs. Stir this into the soaked fruit and fold in the dry ingredients until fully combined.

Grease the base and sides of two 1.25 litre (44 fl oz/5 cup) pudding basins with melted butter. Place a round of baking paper in the base of the bowls. Put the empty bowls in two large saucepans on a trivet or upturned saucer and pour enough cold water into the saucepan to come halfway up the sides of the bowls. Remove the bowls and put the water on to boil.

Spoon the mixture into the pudding bowls. Lay a sheet of foil on the work surface and cover with a sheet of baking paper. Make a large pleat in the middle, then grease the paper with melted butter. Place, paper side down, across the top of one of the bowls and tie string securely around the rim of the bowl and over the top to make a handle. The string handle is used to lift the pudding in and out of the pan. Repeat with the second pudding bowl. Gently lower the bowls into the boiling water, reduce to a fast simmer and cover with a tight-fitting lid. Cook for about 4 hours, checking the water every hour and topping up to the original level with boiling water as needed. Test the puddings with a skewer: if it comes out clean the puddings are ready.

Remove the baking paper and foil and invert the puddings onto a plate. Serve warm with your favourite custard.

tip **This recipe makes two puddings, so if you are only serving one, wrap the other one carefully and store in a dark, cool place for up to 6 months. Re-steam in the pudding bowl for 1 hour on the day of serving.**

Put the fruit, **zests** and nuts in a bowl, then pour on the **beer and rum**.

Tie string securely around the rim of the bowl and over the top to make a **handle**.

double chocolate and potato muffins

makes 12

1 **all-purpose potato**, quartered

125 g (4 1/2 oz) **butter**

150 g (5 1/2 oz/heaped 2/3 cup) **caster (superfine) sugar**

2 **eggs**, lightly beaten

125 g (4 1/2 oz/1/2 cup) **sour cream**

100 g (3 1/2 oz/heaped 1/2 cup) **dark chocolate chips**

125 g (4 1/2 oz/1 cup) **self-raising flour**

85 g (3 oz/2/3 cup) **plain (all-purpose) flour**

1/2 teaspoon **bicarbonate of soda (baking soda)**

30 g (1 oz/1/4 cup) **unsweetened cocoa powder**

4 tablespoons **milk**

Put the potato in a steamer and cover with a lid. Sit the steamer over a saucepan or wok of boiling water and steam for 15–20 minutes, or until tender. Remove and mash with the back of a fork.

Preheat the oven to 170°C (325°F/Gas 3). Lightly grease a 12-hole standard muffin tin, or line with paper muffin cases. Line the outside of the muffin tin with strong foil, covering the bottom and sides with one large piece (this is to protect the muffins from the water bath).

Using electric beaters, cream the butter and sugar in a bowl until light and fluffy. Add the egg gradually, beating well after each addition. Stir in the sour cream, then add the mashed potato and stir until well combined. Add the chocolate chips.

Sift the flours, bicarbonate of soda and cocoa powder into a separate bowl. Add the flour mixture alternately with the milk to the potato mixture, taking care not to overmix as this will produce tough muffins. Spoon the mixture into the muffin holes, filling them three-quarters full, and place in a roasting tin. Pour hot water into the tin to come halfway up the sides of the muffin tin. Bake for 30–40 minutes, or until a skewer comes out clean when inserted into the centre. Check the water level once during cooking, and top up with hot water if necessary.

Carefully remove the muffin tin from the water bath and set aside for 5 minutes before transferring the muffins to a wire rack to cool.

pumpkin and fig cake

serves 10–12

300 g (10½ oz) **pumpkin (winter squash)**, peeled, seeded and cut into 3 cm (1¼ inch) pieces
250 g (9 oz) **butter**, at room temperature
115 g (4 oz/½ cup) **caster (superfine) sugar**
2 **eggs**, lightly beaten
1 tablespoon **maple syrup**
185 g (6½ oz/1 cup) finely chopped **dried figs**
30 g (1 oz/½ cup) **shredded coconut**
½ teaspoon freshly grated **nutmeg**
1 teaspoon **ground cloves**
2 teaspoons **ground cinnamon**
250 g (9 oz/2 cups) **self-raising flour**, sifted
125 ml (4 fl oz/½ cup) **milk**

Line the **outside** of the tin with strong foil to protect the cake from the **water bath**.

Gently fold in the **figs**, **coconut** and cooked **pumpkin**.

Line a steamer with baking paper and punch with holes. Arrange the pumpkin in the steamer and cover with a lid. Sit the steamer over a saucepan or wok of boiling water and steam for 15 minutes, or until tender. Remove and mash the pumpkin with the back of a fork.

Preheat the oven to 180°C (350°F/Gas 4). Lightly grease and line the base and sides of an 18 cm (7 inch) square cake tin. Line the outside of the tin with strong foil, covering the bottom and sides with one large piece (this will protect the cake from the water bath).

Using electric beaters, cream the butter and sugar in a large bowl until light and fluffy. Add the egg and maple syrup gradually, beating well after each addition. Using a large metal spoon or rubber spatula, gently fold in the figs, coconut and cooked pumpkin. Fold in the nutmeg, cloves, cinnamon, half the flour and half the milk. Once combined, add the remaining flour and milk, taking care not to overmix.

Spoon the mixture into the cake tin and place in a roasting tin. Pour hot water into the roasting tin to come halfway up the sides of the cake tin. Cook in the oven for 1 hour 15 minutes, or until a skewer comes out clean when inserted into the centre. If the cake starts to brown too quickly, cover it with foil for the rest of the cooking time. Check the water level every 30 minutes during cooking, and top up with hot water if necessary.

Carefully remove the cake tin from the water bath and set aside for 10 minutes, then transfer the cake to a wire rack to cool.

tip **This cake will keep in an airtight container for up to a week.**

ginger and grapefruit puddings with mascarpone cream

serves 6

1 large **ruby grapefruit**
40 g (1 1/2 oz/1/3 cup) **stem ginger in syrup**, drained and finely chopped, plus 3 teaspoons syrup
1 1/2 tablespoons **golden syrup** or **dark corn syrup**
125 g (4 1/2 oz) **unsalted butter**, softened
115 g (4 oz/1/2 cup) **caster (superfine) sugar**
2 **eggs**, at room temperature
185 g (6 1/2 oz/1 1/2 cups) **self-raising flour**
1 teaspoon **ground ginger**
4 tablespoons **milk**

mascarpone cream

125 g (4 1/2 oz/heaped 1/2 cup) **mascarpone cheese**
125 ml (4 fl oz/1/2 cup) **cream (whipping)**
1 tablespoon **icing (confectioners') sugar**, sifted

Preheat the oven to 170°C (325°F/Gas 3). Grease six 170 ml (5 1/2 fl oz/2/3 cup) pudding basins (moulds) or ramekins.

Finely grate 2 teaspoons of zest from the grapefruit. Slice the grapefruit around its circumference, one-third of the way down. Peel the larger piece, removing any white pith, and cut the flesh into six 1 cm (1/2 inch) slices. Squeeze 3 teaspoons of juice from the remaining grapefruit. Combine the juice, ginger syrup and golden syrup in a bowl. Spoon the mixture into the basins and top with a slice of grapefruit.

Beat the butter and sugar with electric beaters until pale and smooth. Beat in the eggs, one at a time. Sift in the flour and ground ginger, add the milk, grapefruit zest and chopped ginger and mix well. Divide the mixture among the basins. Cover each basin with foil and put them in a deep roasting tin. Pour in enough boiling water to come halfway up the side of the basins. Cover the roasting tin with foil, sealing the edges well. Bake the puddings for 30–35 minutes, or until set.

To make the mascarpone cream, combine the ingredients in a bowl until smooth.

To serve, gently invert the puddings onto serving plates and serve warm with a good dollop of mascarpone cream.

pears with rosé jelly and citrus syrup

serves 6

rosé jelly (gelatin dessert)

600 ml (21 fl oz) **rosé wine**

225 g (8 oz/1 cup) **caster (superfine) sugar**

2 1/2 tablespoons powdered **gelatine**

6 small **pears**

1 **star anise**

1 **cinnamon stick**

8 **cardamom pods**

8 whole **cloves**

citrus syrup

225 g (8 oz/1 cup) **caster (superfine) sugar**

1 teaspoon grated **lime zest**

1 tablespoon **lime juice**

1 teaspoon grated **orange zest**

1 tablespoon **orange juice**

To make the rosé jelly, put the wine in a saucepan and bring to the boil. Remove the pan from the heat and stir in the sugar until it has dissolved. Put the gelatine in a glass bowl, pour in 250 ml (9 fl oz/1 cup) of the heated wine, and stir briskly with a fork until dissolved. Stir in the remaining wine, then pour into six 125 ml (4 fl oz/ 1/2 cup) moulds. Allow to cool, then refrigerate for 3–4 hours, or until set.

Peel and core the pears, leaving the stem on. Cut across the bottom of each pear so they stand up in the steamer. Half-fill a saucepan or wok with water and add the star anise, cinnamon, cardamom and cloves. Bring the water to the boil, then reduce the heat and keep at a rapid simmer. Stand the pears in a steamer in a single layer and cover with a lid. Sit the steamer over the saucepan and steam for 15 minutes, or until a skewer can be inserted with ease all the way through.

Meanwhile, to make the syrup, combine the sugar and 250 ml (9 fl oz/1 cup) of water in a small saucepan and stir over low heat until the sugar has dissolved. Add the citrus zests and juices, bring to the boil, then reduce the heat and simmer without stirring for 10–15 minutes. Take the pan off the heat. Remove the pears from the steamer and put them in the warm citrus syrup while plating up the jelly.

To serve, dip the moulds in hot water for a few seconds. Place a plate on top and turn out the jelly. Serve immediately with the steamed pears and a generous drizzle of the citrus syrup.

vanilla custards with berries

makes 6

375 ml (13 fl oz/1 1/2 cups) **milk**

250 ml (9 fl oz/1 cup) **cream (whipping)**

1 **vanilla bean**, split, seeds scraped

175 g (6 oz/3/4 cup) **caster (superfine) sugar**

3 **eggs**, plus 4 **egg yolks**

150 g (5 1/2 oz/1 1/4 cups) **raspberries**

150 g (5 1/2 oz/1 cup) **blueberries**

250 g (9 oz/1 2/3 cups) small **strawberries**, halved if too large

2 tablespoons **caster (superfine) sugar**, extra

Preheat the oven to 160°C (315°F/Gas 2–3) and grease six 185 ml (6 fl oz/3/4 cup) ramekins. Line a roasting tin with a tea towel (dish towel), then place the ramekins in the tin.

Combine the milk, cream and vanilla bean and seeds in a saucepan over medium heat and bring to the boil. Remove from the heat and set aside. Put the sugar, eggs and yolks in a bowl and whisk until smooth, then slowly whisk in the hot milk mixture. Strain through a fine sieve into a measuring cup then pour the custard evenly into the ramekins.

Pour enough hot water into the roasting tin to come halfway up the sides of the ramekins. Bake for 45 minutes, or until just firm. Remove the ramekins from the tin and cool to room temperature. Cover with plastic wrap and refrigerate overnight.

Combine the raspberries, blueberries and strawberries in a saucepan and sprinkle with the extra sugar. Place over medium heat and toss for 3 minutes, or until the sugar has dissolved and the berries are shiny. Remove from the heat.

To serve, place the ramekins in a pan of hot water for 1 minute to make them easier to unmould. Invert each ramekin onto a plate, then spoon the berries over the custards and serve immediately.

pear and pecan dessert cake

serves 6–8

50 g (1 3/4 oz/1/2 cup) **pecans**

300 g (10 1/2 oz) **dried pears**

150 g (5 1/2 oz) **unsalted butter**

175 g (6 oz/3/4 cup) **caster (superfine) sugar**

1 teaspoon **natural vanilla extract**

3 **eggs**

185 g (6 1/2 oz/1 1/2 cups) **plain (all-purpose) flour**

2 teaspoons **baking powder**

1/2 teaspoon **ground cinnamon**

1/2 teaspoon **ground ginger**

2 tablespoons **milk**

whipped cream, to serve

brown sugar syrup

150 g (5 1/2 oz/2/3 cup) **soft brown sugar**

1 teaspoon **ground cinnamon**

4 tablespoons **brandy**

60 g (2 1/4 oz) **unsalted butter**, softened

Preheat the oven to 180°C (350°F/Gas 4). Grease and line a 24 cm (9 1/2 inch) round cake tin, then arrange the pecans in the base of the tin.

Cover the dried pears with warm water and leave for about 10–15 minutes, or until softened. Pat dry with paper towels.

Using electric beaters, beat the butter and sugar until light and fluffy. Add the vanilla and the eggs one at a time, beating well after each addition. Sift the flour, baking powder, cinnamon and ginger into a bowl, add to the cake mixture and beat slowly to combine. Add the milk and beat for a further minute.

To make the brown sugar syrup, combine the sugar, cinnamon, brandy and butter in a small saucepan over medium heat and cook for 3 minutes, or until the sugar has dissolved.

Pour the warm syrup over the nuts in the cake tin. Arrange the pears over the nuts. Spoon the cake mixture over the pears and smooth the surface with a spatula. Cover the cake tin with a large square of foil, then place the cake tin a large roasting tin. Pour in enough hot water to come halfway up the side of the cake tin, then bake for 40 minutes. Remove the foil and bake for a further 15 minutes, or until golden and cooked through when tested with a skewer.

Leave the cake in the tin for 5 minutes, then carefully invert onto a plate and serve warm with whipped cream.

Spoon the **cake** mixture over the pears and smooth the **surface**.

Pour in enough **hot water** to come halfway up the side of the cake tin.

couscous and apricot pudding

serves 6

90 g (3 1/4 oz/1/2 cup) **dried apricots**, chopped

875 ml (30 fl oz/3 1/2 cups) **apricot nectar**

1 tablespoon grated **lemon zest**

1 **vanilla bean**, split, seeds scraped

1 **cinnamon stick**

1/4 teaspoon **ground cloves**

1 tablespoon **lemon juice**

185 g (6 1/2 oz/1 cup) **couscous**

custard, to serve

Grease six 250 ml (9 fl oz/1 cup) pudding bowls or ovenproof teacups and place a round of baking paper in the bottom of each. Combine the apricots, nectar, lemon zest, vanilla bean and seeds and cinnamon stick in a saucepan over medium heat and bring to the boil. Reduce the heat and simmer for 5 minutes, then remove from the heat and leave for 5 minutes. Strain, reserving the apricots and discarding the vanilla bean and cinnamon stick. Return the nectar to the saucepan and divide the apricots among the pudding bowls.

Add the cloves, lemon juice and couscous to the reserved apricot nectar. Bring to the boil, then reduce the heat to low and simmer, covered, for 8–10 minutes, or until most of the liquid has been absorbed. The mixture should still be quite wet.

Spoon the couscous into the pudding bowls, level the top and cover each with a round of foil. Place the bowls in a steamer and cover with a lid. Sit the steamer over a saucepan or wok of boiling water and steam for 30 minutes, checking the water level regularly.

To serve, turn the puddings out of the bowls and serve hot with custard.

chocolate hazelnut cake with coffee crunch cream

serves 8

125 g (4 1/2 oz) **butter**, softened
280 g (10 oz/1 1/4 cups) **caster (superfine) sugar**
3 **eggs**
60 g (2 1/4 oz/1/2 cup) **plain (all-purpose) flour**
30 g (1 oz/1/4 cup) **self-raising flour**
30 g (1 oz/1/4 cup) **unsweetened cocoa powder**
55 g (2 oz/1/2 cup) **ground hazelnuts**
125 ml (4 fl oz/1/2 cup) **milk**

coffee crunch cream

1 tablespoon **instant coffee granules** (or 1 tablespoon **espresso**)
250 ml (9 fl oz/1 cup) **thickened (whipping) cream**
8 **amaretti biscuits (cookies)**, chopped
1 1/2–2 tablespoons **icing (confectioners') sugar**

Line the base and into the corners of a 23 cm (9 inch) steamer with baking paper. Pleat the paper up the sides and allow the paper to overlap the top edges. Spray or brush with olive oil.

Using electric beaters, beat the butter and sugar in a small bowl until creamy. Add the eggs one at a time, beating well between additions. Transfer to a large bowl.

Sift in the flours and cocoa, add the hazelnuts and milk, and stir to combine. Pour the mixture into the steamer and cover with a lid. Sit the steamer over a saucepan or wok of boiling water and steam for 35–40 minutes, or until the cake is firm in the centre. Lift the cake out of the steamer and cool on a wire rack.

To make the coffee crunch cream, dissolve the coffee in 1 tablespoon of hot water, then cool. Beat the cream with electric beaters until soft peaks form. Stir in the coffee, biscuits and icing sugar, to taste. Spread over the cooled cake and serve.

tip **The coffee crunch cream can be made 2 hours ahead, after which time the biscuits will lose their 'crunch'.**

lime cakes with blackberries

serves 4

185 g (6 1/2 oz/1 1/2 cups) **self-raising flour**
1/2 teaspoon **baking powder**
55 g (2 oz/1/4 cup) **caster (superfine) sugar**
grated zest of 1 **lime**
2 **eggs**
185 ml (6 fl oz/3/4 cup) **buttermilk**
20 g (3/4 oz) **butter**, melted
thick (double/heavy) cream, to serve

blackberry sauce
300 g (10 1/2 oz/scant 1 1/3 cups) **caster (superfine) sugar**
1 tablespoon **lime juice**
1 tablespoon **raspberry liqueur** (optional)
150 g (5 1/2 oz/1 cup) **blackberries**

Grease four 250 ml (9 fl oz/1 cup) rum baba tins or ramekins. Sift the flour and baking powder into a large bowl and mix in the sugar and lime zest. Make a well in the centre, add the eggs and buttermilk and whisk until combined. Stir in the melted butter.

Spoon the mixture into the prepared tins. Place a piece of greased baking paper over the top of each, then wrap tightly in foil.

Place the tins in a steamer and cover with a lid. Sit the steamer over a saucepan or wok of boiling water and steam for 20 minutes, or until risen and firm to the touch.

To make the blackberry sauce, combine the sugar and 200 ml (7 fl oz) of water in a saucepan over low heat and stir until the sugar has dissolved. Bring to the boil, then reduce the heat and simmer without stirring for 15–20 minutes, or until slightly thickened. Add the lime juice, liqueur and blackberries and simmer gently for 5 minutes, or until the syrup takes on the colour of the blackberries. Cool slightly.

Turn the puddings out onto individual plates and spoon the fruit and syrup over the top. Serve hot with cream.

chocolate fudge puddings

serves 8

150 g (5 1/2 oz) **unsalted butter**

175 g (6 oz/3/4 cup) **caster (superfine) sugar**

100 g (3 1/2 oz) **dark chocolate**, melted and cooled (see tip)

2 **eggs**

60 g (2 1/4 oz/1/2 cup) **plain (all-purpose) flour**

90 g (3 1/4 oz/3/4 cup) **self-raising flour**

30 g (1 oz/1/4 cup) **unsweetened cocoa powder**

1 teaspoon **bicarbonate of soda (baking soda)**

125 ml (4 fl oz/1/2 cup) **milk**

whipped cream, to serve

sauce

50 g (1 3/4 oz) **unsalted butter**, chopped

125 g (4 1/2 oz) **dark chocolate**, chopped

125 ml (4 fl oz/1/2 cup) **cream (whipping)**

1 teaspoon **natural vanilla extract**

Half-fill the ramekins or **tea cups** with the chocolate mixture.

Stir the sauce over low heat until the butter and **chocolate** have completely **melted**.

Preheat the oven to 180°C (350°F/Gas 4). Lightly grease eight 250 ml (9 fl oz/1 cup) ramekins or ovenproof tea cups.

Using electric beaters, beat the butter and sugar until light and creamy. Add the melted chocolate, beating well. Add the eggs one at a time, beating well after each addition.

Sift together the flours, cocoa and bicarbonate of soda, then gently fold into the chocolate mixture. Add the milk and fold through. Half-fill the ramekins, then cover with pieces of greased foil and place in a large, deep roasting tin. Pour in enough hot water to come halfway up the sides of the ramekins. Bake for 35–40 minutes, or until a skewer inserted into the centre of each pudding comes out clean.

To make the sauce, combine the butter, chocolate, cream and vanilla in a saucepan and stir over low heat until the butter and chocolate have completely melted. Pour over the puddings and serve with whipped cream.

tip **To melt chocolate, cut it into cubes and place in a heatproof bowl. Sit the bowl over a saucepan of simmering water, making sure the water does not touch the base, and stir with a metal spoon until melted.**

sticky date puddings

serves 6

185 g (6 1/2 oz/1 cup) pitted **dates**, roughly chopped
1 teaspoon **bicarbonate of soda (baking soda)**
70 g (2 1/2 oz) **unsalted butter**, softened
150 g (5 1/2 oz/2/3 cup) **soft brown sugar**
1 teaspoon **natural vanilla extract**
2 **eggs**
150 g (5 1/2 oz/1 1/4 cups) **self-raising flour**, sifted
100 g (3 1/2 oz/1 cup) **walnut halves**, roughly chopped

caramel sauce

155 g (5 1/2 oz/2/3 cup) **soft brown sugar**
60 g (2 1/4 oz) **unsalted butter**
250 ml (9 fl oz/1 cup) **cream (whipping)**

Preheat the oven to 180°C (350°F/Gas 4). Brush six 250 ml (9 fl oz/1 cup) ramekins with melted butter and line the bases with rounds of baking paper. Put the dates, bicarbonate of soda and 250 ml (9 fl oz/1 cup) of water in a saucepan, bring to the boil, then remove from the heat and leave to cool (the mixture will become foamy).

Using electric beaters, beat the butter, sugar and vanilla until light and creamy. Add 1 egg, beat well then fold in 1 tablespoon of the flour. Add the other egg and repeat the process. Fold in the remaining flour, walnuts and date mixture, and mix well. Spoon the mixture into the ramekins.

Arrange the ramekins in a large roasting tin, then pour enough hot water into the tin to come halfway up the sides of the ramekins. Cover with foil and bake for about 35–40 minutes, or until slightly risen and firm to the touch.

To make the caramel sauce, combine the brown sugar, butter and cream in a saucepan over low heat and simmer for 5 minutes, or until the sugar has dissolved.

Loosen the side of each pudding with a small knife, turn out onto serving plates and remove the baking paper. Pour the sauce over the top and serve.

blackberry puddings with crème anglaise

serves 8

125 g (4 1/2 oz) **unsalted butter**, softened

125 g (4 1/2 oz/heaped 1/2 cup) **caster (superfine) sugar**

2 **eggs**, at room temperature

125 g (4 1/2 oz/1 cup) **self-raising flour**

2 tablespoons **milk**

250 g (9 oz/2 1/4 cups) **blackberries**

crème anglaise

325 ml (11 fl oz) **milk**

4 **egg yolks**, at room temperature

80 g (2 3/4 oz/1/3 cup) **caster (superfine) sugar**

Preheat the oven to 180°C (350°F/Gas 4) and grease eight 125 ml (4 fl oz/1/2 cup) dariole moulds.

Using electric beaters, cream the butter and sugar together until light and fluffy. Add the eggs, one at time, beating well after each addition. Sift the flour and gently fold in with enough milk to form a dropping consistency.

Cover the base of each mould with a layer of blackberries. Spoon enough of the pudding mixture over the berries so that the moulds are three-quarters full. Cover the moulds with foil, sealing tightly. Place the puddings in a roasting tin and pour in enough hot water to come halfway up the sides of the moulds. Bake for about 30–35 minutes, or until the puddings spring back when lightly touched.

Meanwhile, to make the crème anglaise, heat the milk to just below boiling point, then set aside. Beat the egg yolks and sugar with electric beaters until thick and pale. Slowly whisk in the hot milk and pour the mixture into a saucepan. Cook over low heat, stirring constantly, for 5–7 minutes, or until the custard is thick enough to coat the back of a spoon. Remove from the heat.

To serve, unmould the puddings onto plates and drizzle with the crème anglaise.

index

Published by Murdoch Books Pty Limited

Murdoch Books Australia
Pier 8/9, 23 Hickson Road, Millers Point NSW 2000
Phone: +61 (0) 2 8220 2000 Fax: +61 (0) 2 8220 2558
www.murdochbooks.com.au

Murdoch Books UK Limited
Erico House, 6th Floor North, 93–99 Upper Richmond Road
Putney, London SW15 2TG
Phone: + 44 (0) 20 8785 5995 Fax: + 44 (0) 20 8785 5985

Chief Executive: Juliet Rogers
Publisher: Kay Scarlett

Concept and art direction: Vivien Valk
Project manager: Janine Flew
Photographer: Ian Hofstetter
Stylist: Jane Collins
Food preparation: Joanne Kelly
Editor: Rachel Carter
Food editor: Wendy Quisumbing
Designer: Susanne Geppert
Recipes by: Wendy Berecry, Grace Campbell, Michelle Earl, Jo Glynn, Katy Holder
Lee Husband, Georgina Leonard, Julie Ray, Mandy Sinclair
Production: Adele Troeger

National Library of Australia Cataloguing-in-Publication Data: Steam it. Includes index.
ISBN 1 74045 638 6. 1. Steaming (cookery).
(Series: It series (Sydney, N.S.W.)). 641.73

Printed by Sing Cheong Printing Co. Ltd in 2006. PRINTED IN HONG KONG.

IMPORTANT: Those who might be at risk from the effects of salmonella poisoning (the elderly, pregnant women, young children and those suffering from immune deficiency diseases) should consult their doctor with any concerns about eating raw eggs.

The publisher would like to thank Cambodia House, Dinosaur Designs and Travellers and Traders for their assistance in the photography for this book.